Mastering

Banking

Macmillan Master Series

Accounting
Arabic
Astronomy
Background to Business
Banking
Basic Management
Biology
British Politics
Business Communication
Business Law
Business Microcomputing
C Programming
Catering Science
Catering Theory
Chemistry
COBOL Programming
Commerce
Computer Programming
Computers
Economic and Social History
Economics
Electrical Engineering
Electronics
English as a Foreign Language
English Grammar
English Language
English Literature
French 1
French 2
German 1
German 2

Hairdressing
Human Biology
Italian 1
Italian 2
Japanese
Keyboarding
Manufacturing
Marketing
Mathematics
Mathematics for Electrical and Electronic
  Engineering
Modern British History
Modern European History
Modern World History
Pascal Programming
Philosophy
Physics
Psychology
Restaurant Service
Science
Secretarial Procedures
Social Welfare
Sociology
Spanish 1
Spanish 2
Spreadsheets
Statistics
Study Skills
Word Processing

Other books by the same author

Elements of Banking
Finance of Foreign Trade
Finance of International Trade
International Trade and Payments
Work Out Elements of Banking
Trade Finance – Payments and Services
  (*joint author with J. Beecham*)

Mastering

Banking

Second Edition

D.P. Whiting

MACMILLAN

First edition 1985
Reprinted twice
Second edition 1994

Published by
THE MACMILLAN PRESS LTD
Houndmills, Basingstoke, Hampshire RG21 2XS
and London
Companies and representatives
throughout the world

ISBN 0–333–59571–8

A catalogue record for this book is available
from the British Library.

Printed in China

10   9   8   7   6   5   4   3   2   1
03   02   01   00   99   98   97   96   95   94

Contents

List of figures

Preface

Since the first edition of this book was published in 1985 there have been very considerable changes in banking and also in banking qualifications, and therefore this second edition amounts to a major reconstruction. The order and structure of the chapters have been changed to bring them in line with the requirements of the Banking Certificate *Business of Banking* syllabus rather than the old *Elements of Banking* syllabus. All of the examination questions used have been taken from past Business of Banking papers.

Whilst the book has been written around the examination syllabus, it is nevertheless meant as a general basic book on banking which should appeal to a wide range of readers who wish to know the basic facts about the subject. This includes those who are planning to become qualified under the National Vocational Qualifications scheme and who will be tested for their practical abilities as bankers; but who, nevertheless, will need to have the necessary knowledge of the banking system and the law and regulations that govern it, if they are to carry out their practical duties efficiently.

As I mentioned in the preface to the first edition, the general reader should find much of interest in this book. A knowledge of the UK financial system is becoming more and more desirable for people in most walks of life, and the subject of banking has progressed a great deal from being a 'stuffy' one to being a topic that is very relevant to our modern way of life.

Wherever possible I have used both masculine and feminine gender in this book, but at times it would have seemed very tedious to do so, and therefore I ask for the indulgence of lady readers. Wherever the masculine gender only has been used it is meant to include the feminine as well.

I am most grateful to Mr Brian Rawle, Director of Studies at the Chartered Institute of Bankers, for his permission to reproduce the examination questions, and to him and to Mr Don Voysey, for their help and advice concerning the chapter on Banking Qualifications. My sincere thanks also go to Mr David Butcher for his help on the use of plastic cards and for advising me on the finer points about wordprocessing.

D.P. Whiting

Acknowledgements

The author and publishers wish to thank the following for permission to reproduce copyright material: Access Brand Ltd; Bank of England; Banking World; Barclaycard; J. Allan Cash Ltd; Eurocard; Eurocheque; General Motors; International Stock Exchange; Lloyds Bank Ltd; Luncheon Vouchers Ltd; Marks & Spencer; Mercury Communications; Metropolitan Bank; National Savings; National Westminster Bank; Nationwide Building Society; Pearl Assurance; Post Office; Gordon Roberts.

List of statutes

List of cases

List of abbreviations

ACIB	Associate Member of the Chartered Institute of Bankers
APACS	Association of Payment Clearing Services
APR	Annual percent age rate
ATM	Automated teller machine
BACS	Bankers' Automated Services Ltd, now known as BACS Ltd
Cert ACIB	Holder of the Banking Certificate of the Chartered Institute of Bankers
CHAPS	Clearing House Automated Payment Services
Dip FS	Diploma in Financial Services of the Chartered Institute of Bankers
EFTPOS	Electronic Funds Transfer – Point of Sale
FIMBRA	Financial Intermediaries, Managers and Brokers' Regulatory Association
IMRO	Investment Management Regulatory Organisation
LAUTRO	Life Assurance and Unit Trust Regulatory Organisation
MO	Official measure of the monetary base, i.e. notes and coin and bank balances at the Bank of England
M2	A wider measure of the money supply – includes MO plus bank and building society current deposits
M4	Broader than M2 – it includes all deposits irrespective of their size and the amount of notice required for withdrawals
MBA	Master in Business Administration
NVQ	National Vocational Qualification
PEP	Personal Equity Plan
PIN	Personal Identification Number
SWIFT	Society for Worldwide Interbank Financial Telecommunication
TESSA	Tax Exempt Special Savings Account
TSA	The Securities Association – all members of the Stock Exchange are members
TSB	Trustee Savings Bank – now known as TSB Bank plc

1 Money

1.1   Introduction

In order to fully appreciate the importance of the banking system within the economy, it is necessary to consider the functions of money, and what constitutes 'money' in modern UK society. The size of the money supply and the methods of controlling it have become highly important factors to governments in pursuing their economic policies. As we shall see, bank deposits account for the majority of the UK money supply, and therefore control over the ability of the banks to create new deposits is essential if the money supply is to be controlled.

1.2   Barter and its Problems

The exchange of goods

If we were all self-sufficient and preferred not to trade with one another there would be no need for money. In a primitive society this might be possible, of

Figure 1.1   Barter

course, but it is inconceivable that we could live like this today even in the small communes that are established from time to time. Some **direct** exchange of goods – barter – is likely to be inevitable, and if trading becomes at all extensive then barter must give way to **indirect** exchange involving the use of money.

Barter means the direct exchange of goods one for another, and it does not require much imagination to see that an immediate problem comes to the fore once two people decide to embark on the exchange of goods (see Figure 1.1). This is the measurement of the value of one of the goods in terms of the other. How many units of Commodity **A** must be handed over in exchange for a unit of Commodity **B**? A bargain must be struck by the two parties concerned and if this is a 'one-off' transaction then they will no doubt haggle with one another until they reach an agreement as to what is to be the rate of exchange. If it is one of many similar transactions then the rate of exchange will have already become established by the forces of supply and demand in the market, and the two parties will tend to adhere to the market rate of exchange – the market price. If one of the people concerned holds out for a higher price for his commodity (2 sacks of potatoes for his bag of corn when the market price is $1\frac{1}{2}$ sacks of potatoes) then he is likely to find that the buyer of corn will look for another supplier.

As we shall see, this problem of the terms on which goods shall be exchanged applies not only in barter (direct exchange) but also in indirect exchange as well, when the price of a commodity is not determined in terms of another commodity but in terms of money. There are, however, some problems which apply only to barter and not to indirect exchange. These are outlined below, and it is because of them that barter rarely takes place.

Problems that arise with barter

Indivisibility   Where an individual has a large indivisible commodity, such as a live cow, to dispose of he may experience difficulty in bartering it if only small commodities are offered in exchange. He may end up with a large number of small objects in exchange and then have the problem of disposing of some of them because he has far more than he needs.

Perishable commodities   If an individual takes units of a commodity in exchange for his commodity in excess of his immediate needs and these units are perishable, then an obvious problem arises. How does he store them until they are required or until they can be exchanged for other goods?

Consistency of quality   The lack of quality in some goods, especially live animals, makes it difficult to arrive at a constant and recognised rate of exchange, e.g. 1 sheep equals 3 sacks of corn, so that each such transaction involves striking a fresh bargain.

Double coincidence of wants   This is undoubtedly the biggest problem that arises with barter for unless the person disposing of goods can find someone who needs them and has something to offer in exchange which he in turn needs, the swap is unlikely to take place.

1.3   Functions and Characteristics of Money

Origins of money

So far we have been concerned with barter which involves the direct exchange of goods one for another and, as we have seen, barter has serious drawbacks which make it unsuitable as a method of exchange once trading becomes at all extensive. It is because of these problems with direct exchange that money originated. One commodity which was particularly sought after by the community, and which was reasonably durable and divisible, came to be used as the medium of exchange. Examples of such commodities are shells, salt, spears, cloth and grain, which have all been used at times as a 'money supply'. They were indeed money, because they were acceptable as a means of payment for goods: not ideal forms of money perhaps, but nevertheless that is what they were. Later metals – bronze and copper, followed by silver and gold – were recognised as being ideally suitable as money because they satisfied most of the necessary characteristics of money. Because they were valuable only small quantities of these metals were required when paying for goods; they were durable; and, what is particularly important, they could be cut, weighed and marked and recognised as units of particular value. More about this later, but in the meantime we must look more closely at the functions and characteristics of money.

Functions of money

There are four functions of money as distinct from the characteristics (the necessary qualities) of money and it is important that you should memorise and understand them. The functions of money are as follows:

- Medium of exchange
- Unit of account
- Store of value
- Standard for deferred payments

Medium of exchange   Money is used as a means of indirect exchange, as we have seen, and therefore one of its functions must be to act as a medium of exchange. In order to fulfil this function money must be acceptable to those who have goods and services to sell. To be acceptable it must be reasonably stable in value so that the holder knows that he will be able to obtain roughly the same quantity of goods and services with it when he chooses to spend it, and for this to happen it must be relatively scarce and its quantity controlled. If the money supply is acceptable then anyone who takes it in exchange for goods will do so in the knowledge that others will accept it when the time comes to spend the money. It can safely be kept in the belief that this is so, and that it can be spent as and when the holder chooses to do so.

Unit of account   As a unit of account money acts as a measuring rod, and without this it would be impossible for a modern community to function. It must be possible to measure the value of goods and services in terms of a common unit, in order to establish prices, and in order to record transactions. We must be able to compare the value of the commodity with that of another, and thus to establish which goods we will buy with our limited supply of money. With a unit of account it becomes possible to measure the value of production, and of the national wealth. We have already considered the problems of barter where there is no common unit of account, and it does not require much imagination to understand the difficulties that would ensue if all of our output of goods and services and our total wealth involved adding up a wide range of goods rather than their monetary value. Our gross national product (GNP) would be quoted as so many cars plus so many ships, and so on, instead of so many millions of pounds. Banking would certainly be impossible in such circumstances.

Store of value   The value of money must remain relatively constant, otherwise people would not wish to hold it. That is what is meant by a store of value. Even during periods of rather severe inflation, however, when the value of money has fallen quite rapidly, it has continued to function as money. But there is a limit beyond which confidence in a currency drops so much that the holders of it switch out of money and into commodities as soon as possible. When such a situation gets out of hand, a country is said to have hyperinflation and the consequence is certain to be that the money supply will have to be replaced. This happened in Germany in 1922–3 and in Hungary after the Second World War, and there have been other examples more recently. Until a new form of money is issued, the community will devise its own form of money by using such things as cigarettes as the medium of exchange and unit of account. There may also be a different unit of account for some purposes during such a period in that a foreign currency, e.g. US dollars, may be used as the unit of account for some contracts.

Standard for deferred payments   Money must be a means whereby debts may be measured and recorded and without which all transactions would have to be for cash and there would be no need for banks and other financial institutions. In other words money must be a standard for deferred payments. The majority of transactions between businesses are on credit terms: the supplier sends the goods to the buyer and records the transaction in his books and sends an invoice to the buyer. When the invoice is paid the book debt is paid off. Similarly if an individual buys a car he may pay a deposit and take credit for the remainder under a hire-purchase agreement or maybe a loan from his bank. He then pays off the debt in monthly instalments. Such credit transactions would not be possible if money was not acting as a standard for deferred payments.

You will realise, I am sure, that this function is closely allied to the store of value function in that credit is unlikely to be given if the value of money is depreciating rapidly.

Characteristics of money

Money must have certain characteristics if it is to overcome the difficulties of barter. Make sure that you can distinguish these **characteristics** (or qualities) from the **functions** of money (listed on p. 4). The characteristics of money are as follows:

- Scarcity
- Uniformity and recognisability
- Divisibility
- Portability
- Durability
- Acceptability

Scarcity   This characteristic has already been referred to when considering the function of money as a store of value. The money supply must be relatively scarce, and to this end it is usually controlled by a central authority, i.e. a government department (the Treasury) and/or the central bank. Unless money is limited in supply the community will be able to demand goods and services in excess of their supply and inflation will result. This means that prices will rise in an attempt to equate the demand for goods with the supply, and if prices are rising the value of money is falling. If the value of money falls it is not fulfilling its function as a store of value and therefore may no longer be acceptable as money. Price stability is also of importance in that the lack of it could affect our competitiveness abroad. If our rate of inflation is greater than that of other countries we will find it more difficult to sell our goods in those countries unless we allow the exchange rate (the rate at which our currency is exchanged for that of another country) to fall.

Uniformity and recognisability   Each unit of money must be the same in size and appearance and thus recognised for what it is. Hence, these days, coins for the same amount are uniform (sometimes referred to as homogeneous), i.e. identical, and are marked with their value, and similarly bank notes are readily identifiable by their size and what is printed on them.

Even intangible forms of money, such as bank and building society deposits, must be uniform in that they must be on a current or cheque-bearing account and must be with a reputable and recognisable deposit-taker, if they are to be acceptable as a means of payment. We will be looking at this form of money later, when we shall see that it is the cheque or piece of plastic used to withdraw a deposit which has to be acceptable rather than the deposit itself.

Divisibility   The unit of account, for instance the pound sterling, must be easily divisible in order that change may be given for transactions involving odd amounts. For this reason coins, or possibly bank notes, are issued for various small amounts such as the 1p, 2p, 5p, 10p, 20p, 50p and £1 coins with which we are familiar. Similarly notes are issued for larger sums than the £1 unit of account, so that payments can be more easily made for varying amounts of money. In some countries such as Italy the value of the unit of account is so small (the Italian lira) that it is not necessary for coins or notes to be issued for small amounts.

When bank deposits are used as money the cheque (or other means of payment) can be made out for the precise amount, e.g. £179.75, and no change is necessary.

Portability   In modern times it would not be convenient for large forms of money to be used, such as the bags of grain used under the barter system, because they are not portable. All modern forms of money are easily portable, though even today we hear complaints about the inconvenience of carrying more than a small number of the £1 coins about. If a unit of account depreciates rapidly there will possibly come a time when it will need to be replaced with a new unit (the new franc or the new lira) worth maybe 10 times or 100 times the value of the old unit. Otherwise considerable quantities of notes have to be carried about in order to pay even relatively small amounts.

For the supermarket holding and transporting large quantities of notes and coins can be risky and also expensive in terms of labour, and therefore the use of plastic means of payment has been encouraged by them. Some supermarkets even offer to supply their customers with bank notes when they use a Switch card, or similar card, as a means of payment, i.e. they add the amount of the cash to the bill for the goods being purchased.

Durability   In contrast to some of the commodities used as money under the barter system, modern forms of money are far more durable and this must be so if the money supply is to be used to cover the very large volume of transactions that take place in our form of society. Our modern coins last for years but when they are worn down they are replaced by new ones. Bank notes are less durable but nevertheless will last for some months, or even years, before they have to be replaced, provided that they are not misused.

Bank deposits and deposits with other financial intermediaries are intangible and do not need to be durable in the same sense as notes and coins. However, they need to be longlasting and continuous if they are to be used by the account holders as a means of exchange.

Acceptability   Money must be acceptable to others if it is to be used as a medium of exchange and in order to be so must have all the other qualities we have already looked at. People must have confidence in the money, or they will not take it. This does not necessarily mean that money must have an intrinsic value equal to its face value. At one time this was always so with gold and silver coins in that the value of each coin was related to an official value for the metal concerned. This is not so today and indeed the value of the alloys that make up a modern coin will be quite insignificant in relation to the token value of the coin marked on the face of it. Similarly, bank notes cost only a fraction of their face value to produce. People have confidence in the notes and coins because they are issued either by the government or by the central bank with government backing. Whether or not a creditor will accept a cheque or plastic card used to transfer a sum of money from a bank or building society deposit will depend a great deal upon his confidence in the bank or building society concerned, as well as his confidence in the ability of the person drawing the cheque to meet it when it is presented for payment.

1.4   Modern Money

The present-day money supply comprises:

- **Coins**
- **Bank notes**
- **Bank deposits**
- **Building society deposits**

Coins

In the UK the coinage is produced by the Royal Mint in quantities directed by the Bank of England. The Chancellor of the Exchequer is Master of the Mint. Coins form the small change in our money supply and therefore their total value is quite small as a proportion of our total money supply and it is limited to the amount that the community needs. If the Bank of England, through which new coins are issued, finds that more coins of a particular denomination are required it will order more, and at the same time it will accept from the other banks coins which are to be demonetised, such as the old 1/2p coin, and also coins that are worn.

Bank notes

The first bankers in Britain were the goldsmiths, who, in addition to their trade as craftsmen in gold and silver, found that they could profit from accepting gold and silver for safe-keeping. They gave receipts for such deposits, and gradually these began to be passed from hand to hand – they were after all issued by well-known and highly-respected goldsmiths who could be trusted to pay over gold and silver coins against receipts should the holders choose to present them.

Consequently the early bankers found that once deposited the gold and silver lodged with them remained intact whilst the evidence of the debts which existed between them and their depositors circulated and rarely came home to roost. They therefore lent some of the coins lodged with them, and charged interest on the loans, and these coins tended to find their way back to the bank as fresh deposits to be lent and re-lent. Clearly this became a very profitable activity, and to encourage holders of their receipts to pass them from hand to hand the gold-smiths started to issue them in convenient denominations, e.g. £1 and £5, and thus the bank note originated.

The goldsmiths then gave up their work as craftsmen, and devoted their time to the development of their banking business. They were followed by other mer-chants in corn and worsted cloth and other commodities who similarly accepted deposits and issued their own notes against them and made advances on the basis that they needed to keep only a proportion of their customers' deposits in gold and silver. Thus the private note issues flourished, and at the beginning of the nineteenth century concern began to be expressed about the size of the note issues, culminating in the Bank Charter Act 1844 which centralised the note issue in the hands of the Bank of England.

Whereas until 1931 the Bank of England's note issue was convertible on demand into gold (this meant that a holder of a bank note could exchange his note for gold at the Bank of England), present-day bank notes are not backed by gold, only by government securities. In reality they are based on confidence – confidence that they will remain acceptable as a means of exchange and, as we have seen, this will greatly depend upon whether the value of the pound remains reasonably constant.

This confidence or trust lies behind the term **fiduciary issue** which is used to describe the Bank of England's present-day note issue. In fact the term 'fidu-ciary' means 'trust'.

The Bank of England's fiduciary note issue has been controlled by a series of Currency and Bank Note Acts under which it has been allowed to increase in line with the needs of the community. This it must do or the banks would be placed in the ludicrous position of having to say to their customers that they could not withdraw their deposits in cash because of a shortage of notes, and could withdraw only by issuing cheques to third parties or paying for goods with plastic cards. At the present time the note issue stands at approximately £15,500 million. This may seem a very large amount but it must be seen in the light of the total money supply. It constitutes only about 5 per cent of the money supply in its narrow sense (M2, see below).

Bank deposits

If you go into a supermarket to buy goods you will have a number of choices as to the means of payment to use at the check-out. You may opt to pay cash (notes and coin), or you may decide to use some of your deposit at your bank by means of a cheque or a debit card or, if the store allows, you may take the goods on credit using the store's own credit card, or that of a credit card company.

Let us leave the use credit cards for now (we will look at them later in this chapter) and concentrate on the use of your bank deposit. You can make use of your deposit either by drawing a cheque on your bank or by using the Switch or Delta card provided by it. In either case you are authorising your bank to transfer some of your deposit to the supermarket. These days you will be encouraged to use your debit card as it is a quick and convenient method and it was in fact designed to be just that (see Section 1.6). Note that it is the bank deposit that is the money supply rather than the cheque or the Switch or Delta card.

Bank deposits are in fact the main part of the money supply and they are a very convenient means of payment, not only to the individual paying for goods in a shop or through the post, but also to the business concern. All businesses use cheques or other ways of transferring bank deposits to settle accounts with one another and the total value of such transactions each year is simply enormous.

It is debatable whether all bank deposits should be regarded as part of the money supply in that they are not all repayable on demand, and this debate is reflected in the various official measures of the money supply (see below). If cheques can be drawn upon a particular bank account then clearly it is part of the money supply and this applies these days to a wide range of accounts – even to some accounts on which interest is paid. Some banks have attracted deposits by offering high interest cheque accounts but they do specify a minimum balance which must be maintained if the interest is to be paid, and it could be argued that that minimum balance is not part of the money supply in that it cannot be readily withdrawn.

If we have money on deposit at a bank we will tend to regard it as virtually cash and will take it into account when calculating our liquidity position (see below). This applies even if we have to give notice of withdrawal and/or will lose some interest if we make the withdrawal. By foresight and good management a customer is able to give notice at the appropriate time in order to withdraw the cash without penalty to meet an anticipated cash requirement. Some banks offer to 'sweep' accounts automatically. This means that where a customer specifies a maximum sum that he wishes to hold on his current account (his cheque account), the bank will transfer any balance in excess of that sum to an interest-bearing account or to a higher interest account, and will be prepared to switch balances back as and when required without a notice period. This plan encourages customers to maintain larger balances with the bank than they might otherwise do and affects the customer's **liquidity**. This concept of liquidity is important because it affects the action of the community in demanding goods and services – the nearer financial assets are to being convertible into cash or cheque account balances the more liquid they are, and the more likely they are to be used to buy goods and services.

Building society deposits

Building societies are institutions that accept deposits from their customers and, in the main, use these to lend money to people buying houses against mortgages (legal charges) on the properties. To a limited extent the societies have been allowed to lend money for other purposes in recent years. The depositors in effect own the building societies as shareholders, but instead of receiving dividends on their investments as they would do if they invested in shares in public companies, they receive interest on their deposits.

There has been fierce competition for customers between the banks and the building societies, and to this end many of the societies now provide cheque accounts to their depositors and offer facilities similar to the banks, such as standing orders and interest on current accounts. One of the main building societies, the Abbey National, became a public company in 1989 and, as such, is now subject to the Banking Acts and is officially a bank. Deposits with the societies must now be regarded as part of the money supply in a similar way to bank deposits, and the official money supply figures make no distinction between the two.

Near-money

The term near-money (sometimes referred to as quasi-money), is used to cover assets which are very nearly part of the money supply but which, because they are not sufficiently liquid, cannot be treated as money (see Figure 1.2). So we are back to the concept of liquidity which we looked at earlier on. Clearly notes and coin and bank and building society deposits are part of the money supply provided that the deposits can be withdrawn on demand by drawing a cheque or by using a bank or building society plastic card to pay for goods or to draw cash at an automated teller machine (ATM). However, there are some bank and building society deposits which cannot be withdrawn without giving a required period of notice such as 3 or 6 months, and these deposits come into the category of near-money rather than money. Indeed one of the factors which determine whether a financial asset is money or near-money is the time factor – whether or not notice of withdrawal has to be given. Another factor is whether or not the asset has to be

Figure 1.2   Near-money

Figure 1.3   Legal tender

converted into cash before it can be used, an example being a postal order which has to be paid for in cash and then presented for payment to the Post Office for payment when cash will be handed over for it. Similarly, securities such as National Savings Certificates and Premium Bonds are encashable at the Post Office, or possibly by warrant through the post. They are registered in the name of the holder and only he or she may give notice of withdrawal, unless the holder is deceased in which case his/her personal representative may demand repayment.

Another factor that applies to near-money is that in some cases a capital loss may have to be borne by the owner should he wish to liquidate the asset. An example of this is stocks and shares. These are normally sold through a security dealer at the market price on the day of sale. Market prices for stocks and shares change from day to day and are based on supply and demand. The investor hopes that having bought some shares he will receive more for them at a later date because of the success of the company in making profits which are passed on to the shareholders as dividends. This does not always happen, of course, especially during a recession, and the holder may have no alternative but to take a loss if he is obliged to sell.

Legal tender

This term is applied to forms of money which must be accepted by law in payment for goods and services (see Figure 1.3). The Coinage Act 1970 lays down that the following constitute legal tender:

- **1p and 2p coins for amounts up to 20p**
- **5p, 10p and 20p coins for amounts up to £5**
- **50p coins for amounts up to £10**
- **£1 coins for any amount**

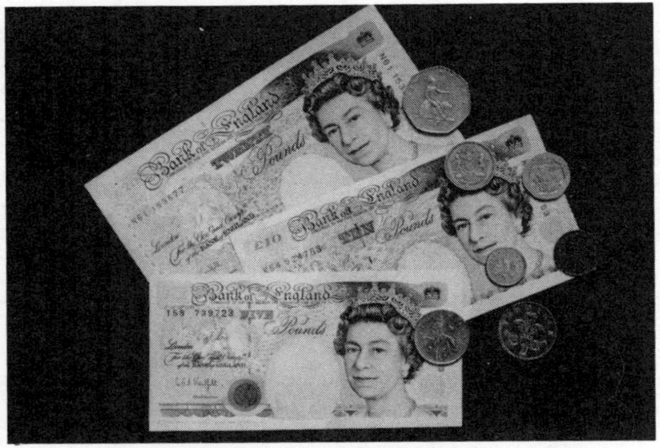

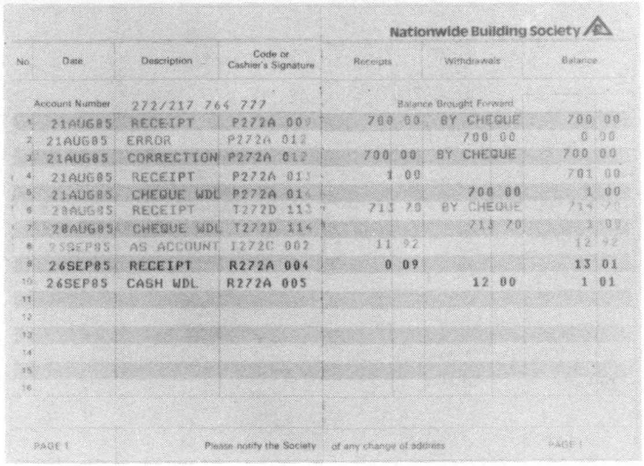

Nationwide Building Society

No.	Date	Description	Code or Cashier's Signature	Receipts	Withdrawals	Balance
	Account Number	272/217 764 777			Balance Brought Forward	
1	21AUG85	RECEIPT	P272A 009	700 00	BY CHEQUE	700 00
2	21AUG85	ERROR	P272A 012		700 00	0 00
3	21AUG85	CORRECTION	P272A 012	700 00	BY CHEQUE	700 00
4	21AUG85	RECEIPT	P272A 013	1 00		701 00
5	21AUG85	CHEQUE WDL	P272A 014		700 00	1 00
6	28AUG85	RECEIPT	T272D 113	713 70	BY CHEQUE	714 70
7	28AUG85	CHEQUE WDL	T272D 114		713 70	1 00
8	25SEP85	AS ACCOUNT	I272C 002	11 92		12 92
9	26SEP85	RECEIPT	R272A 004	0 09		13 01
10	26SEP85	CASH WDL	R272A 005		12 00	1 01
11						
12						
13						
14						
15						
16						

PAGE 1 Please notify the Society of any change of address PAGE 1

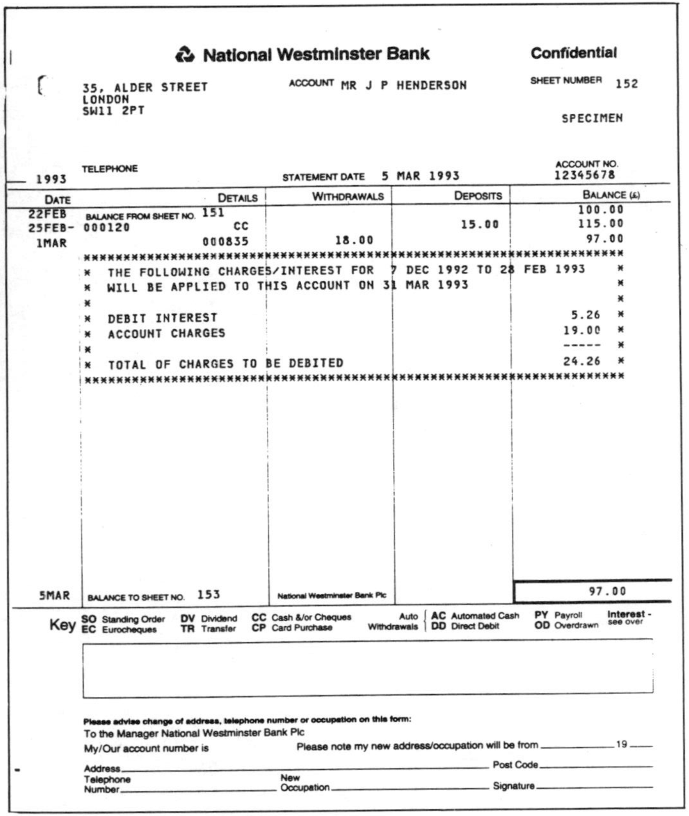

National Westminster Bank Confidential

35, ALDER STREET
LONDON
SW11 2PT

ACCOUNT MR J P HENDERSON

SHEET NUMBER 152

SPECIMEN

1993 TELEPHONE STATEMENT DATE 5 MAR 1993 ACCOUNT NO. 12345678

Date	Details	Withdrawals	Deposits	Balance (£)
22FEB	BALANCE FROM SHEET NO. 151			100.00
25FEB-	000120 CC		15.00	115.00
1MAR	000835	18.00		97.00

****
* THE FOLLOWING CHARGES/INTEREST FOR 7 DEC 1992 TO 28 FEB 1993 *
* WILL BE APPLIED TO THIS ACCOUNT ON 31 MAR 1993 *
*
* DEBIT INTEREST 5.26 *
* ACCOUNT CHARGES 19.00 *
* ----- *
* TOTAL OF CHARGES TO BE DEBITED 24.26 *
****

5MAR BALANCE TO SHEET NO. 153 National Westminster Bank Plc 97.00

Key SO Standing Order EC Eurocheques DV Dividend TR Transfer CC Cash &/or Cheques CP Card Purchase Auto Withdrawals AC Automated Cash DD Direct Debit PY Payroll OD Overdrawn Interest - see over

Please advise change of address, telephone number or occupation on this form:
To the Manager National Westminster Bank Plc
My/Our account number is Please note my new address/occupation will be from ______ 19 ___
Address ______ Post Code ______
Telephone Number ______ New Occupation ______ Signature ______

Figure 1.4 The money supply

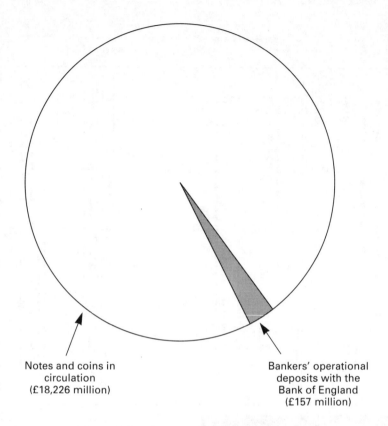

Notes and coins in
circulation
(£18,226 million)

Bankers' operational
deposits with the
Bank of England
(£157 million)

Figure 1.5   The monetary base (M0)
Source: Bank of England Bulletin

In addition to these stipulations in the Act, £5, £10, £20, £50 Bank of England notes are legal tender for any amount.

This does not mean that anyone selling goods is obliged to give change. This is not so because by law the purchaser must tender the precise amount. Therefore, whereas a bus driver/conductor is legally required to accept 20 1p coins for a 20p fare, he is not obliged to change a £5 note for such a fare.

1.5   The Official Money Supply

The government publishes official figures for the UK money supply each month and these are carefully scrutinised by economists and financial journalists for indications as to how successful, or otherwise, the authorities have been in controlling the money stock (see Figure 1.4). During times of inflation the government will be expected to limit the rate of growth of the money supply, whilst during a recession it will allow a more rapid growth in order to stimulate an expansion in the national output of goods and services.

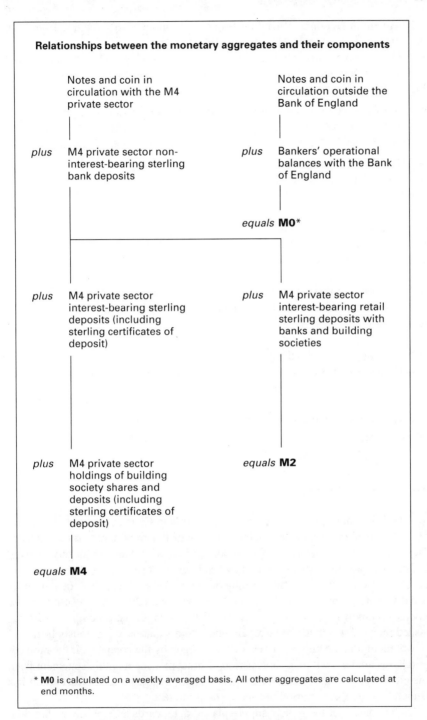

Figure 1.6   Official definitions of money
Source: Bank of England Bulletin (August 1992)

There are in fact three official measures of the money stock ranging from MO, the narrowest measure, to M4, the broadest measure:

● MO   This measures the monetary base, i.e. the money held in the most liquid forms by private individuals and by businesses for day-to-day transactions (see Figure 1.5), as follows:

● Notes and coins in circulation outside the Bank of England, plus bankers' operational balances with the Bank of England (note that the building societies are not required to keep balances with the Bank of England).

● M2   This is another narrow measure of the money supply but it is much broader in that it includes bank and building society deposits as well as notes and coins, as follows:

● Notes and coins in circulation outside the Bank of England
● Private sector non-interest-bearing sterling bank deposits
● Interest-bearing retail sterling deposits with banks and building societies

● M4   This is a much broader measure of the money supply than M2 in that it includes all deposits irrespective of their size and the amount of notice required for withdrawal:

● Notes and coins with the general public
● All deposits in sterling from UK residents with banks and building societies including wholesale deposits

Figure 1.6 shows the relationships between the monetary aggregates M0-M4 and their components.

1.6   Plastic Money

We shall be looking at cheques and cheque cards in Chapter 6 and at plastic and electronic banking in Chapter 10, but at this stage it is important to refer briefly to them in the context of money. We are all familiar with what are loosely referred to as credit cards but which in fact may be either debit cards or credit cards. Debit cards are used to authorise the debiting of the holder's current account and this is usually done within 3 days of a purchase, whilst credit cards are used to buy goods on credit terms by incurring a debt to the credit card company that has issued the card which has to be repaid under terms that have previously been laid down, including the rate of interest that is charged by the company. If the month's purchases are paid within a short period of time after the monthly statement from the credit card company is issued, interest is not charged and in effect credit has been taken for a short period of time without interest.

In the context of the money supply plastic debit cards are not money but, like cheques, are used to transfer the ownership of money, i.e. bank deposits. It is important to understand that it is the bank deposit that is money and not the plastic card. Similarly plastic credit cards are not money but they are a means of borrowing money in the form of the credit card company's bank deposit that is being used to pay for goods by the cardholder.

Plastic cards are also issued by the banks and some building societies as cheque guarantee cards. They can be used by the holder to support a cheque which he has issued and, provided that certain conditions have been met, the retailer is assured of payment up to the limit stipulated on the card (this could be £50, £100 or £250). Neither the plastic card nor the cheque are in fact money, only the bank deposit on which the cheque has been drawn. The customer of the bank or building society may also use the card or, possibly, a special card issued for the purpose, to withdraw cash from an ATM outside the bank or building society or at some other location, such as a supermarket. Here again it is not the card that is money but the bank notes that are drawn from the machine and which are debited to the cardholder's current account. He has swapped some of his bank deposit for cash and will use that cash to make purchases.

Review Questions

1   How would you distinguish between direct exchange and indirect exchange? (1.2)
2   What problems arise with trade by means of barter? (1.2)
3   How did money originate? (1.3)
4   What is meant by a medium of exchange? (1.3)
5   What is meant by a unit of account? (1.3)
6   How would you define a store of value? (1.3)
7   What is a standard for deferred payments? (1.3)
8   What are the essential characteristics of money? List and briefly explain them. (1.3)
9   Which institution is responsible for the coinage in Britain? (1.4)
10   How did bank notes originate? (1.4)
11   What is meant by the fiduciary issue? (1.4)
12   Are Bank of England notes convertible into gold? (1.4)
13   What is the approximate size of the note issue? (1.4)
14   How can a bank deposit be part of the money supply? (1.4)
15   What is meant by a person's liquidity? (1.4)
16   Are building society deposits money? (1.4)
17   What is meant by near-money? Give examples. (1.4)
18   What is meant by legal tender? State the maximum amounts of each coin that must be accepted in payment. (1.4)
19   Is anyone selling goods obliged to give change? (1.4)
20   How would you define M0 (1.5)
21   How would you define M2 (1.5)
22   How would you define M4 (1.5)
23   What is meant by plastic money? (1.6)

Past Examination Questions ────────────

1   (a) List the characteristics of money.   (*4 marks*)

    (b) Using notes or a table show how each of the following forms of
         money either satisfies or does not satisfy the characteristics listed
         in (a):
         (i)   Credit cards
         (ii)   Sea shells
         (iii) Luncheon vouchers.   (*16 marks*)

2   (a) Define the functions of money.   (*8 marks*)

    (b) Explain the effect of high inflation on the ability of money to carry
         out each of these functions.   (*12 marks*)

3   (a) Define legal tender, money and near-/quasi-money.   (*6 marks*)

    (b) State whether each of the following are legal tender, money or
         near-/quasi-money. For each, give two disadvantages to show how
         it fails to meet all the requirements of money:
               50p coin
               Cheque account
               Deposit account
               Credit card   (*14 marks*)

4   Give **four** reasons why barter was replaced by money.
                                               (Part question, *8 marks*)

2 The UK banking system

┌─ **Chapter objectives** ───┐

When you have carefully studied this chapter you should be able to:
- Explain the type, purpose and functions of the financial market place
- Define the purpose and functions of the Bank of England
- Explain what is meant by the retail banks, the merchant banks, and the other banks, and define their functions

└──┘

2.1   Introduction

In this chapter we will examine some of the activities of the banks, including the Bank of England, which together predominate in the financial market. There are many other important institutions which function and play significant roles within the market, and we shall examine these in Chapter 3 and then we shall be able to look at the London Money Market as a whole. The banks and all of the other institutions are financial intermediaries in that they bring together borrowers and lenders in an indirect way. Those with funds to spare deposit them with the banks or in some way invest the funds with institutions in the market, and these funds are lent to others who need to borrow. Those with surplus funds do not lend them directly to those who want to borrow, but instead do so through one or other of the financial intermediaries.

Financial intermediaries take on the time-consuming task of collecting the investments of those with funds to spare, in some cases quite small sums, and aggregate them to provide the large amounts which some borrowers require. Hopefully, the intermediary takes from the investor the risk of loss and is able to balance the need of the lender for early redemption of the loan with the possible long-term needs of the borrower. An investor might not be willing to lend on the basis of a notice of withdrawal of more than, say, 3 months, and yet a financial intermediary is able to agree to that and still lend to someone for a fixed period of, say, 10 years.

In recent years the high street banks have suffered fierce competition from the other financial institutions and have had to adjust their services to take account of this competition. We shall consider this competition as we progress through the rest of this book.

2.2   The Bank of England

The development of the Bank

The Bank of England was established in 1694 with two privileges which the then existing smaller banks did not have. The bank was allowed corporate status and also royal patronage, the latter in response to a loan to the King – William III – who needed funds to fight a war against France. By corporate status we mean that it was a joint stock company with a large number of shareholders and hence it was able to raise a larger amount of capital than the small private banking businesses which from then on, and for 140 years, were not permitted to have more than six partners. In this privileged position the Bank of England flourished and gradually predominated more and more over the other banks. It began as an ordinary bank in the sense that it performed the same functions as the private banks, but over the years assumed the functions which we now attribute to a central bank. In view of its special relationship with the monarch, it assumed the role of the government's bank and as the largest issuer of bank notes was allowed eventually to take over the note issues of all the other banks as the Bank Charter Act 1844 gradually became fully effective. Apart from relatively small local note issues by the banks in Scotland, the Bank of England is now fully responsible for the note issue in Britain.

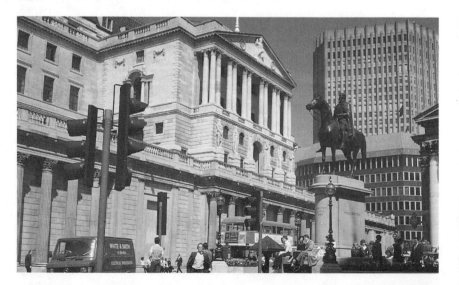

Figure 2.1   The Bank of England ('The Old Lady of Threadneedle Street')

Relationship with other banks

Inasmuch as the Bank of England became the main note-issuing bank and that some of the smaller banks elected to use Bank of England notes rather than issue new notes themselves, the private banks became very dependent upon the Bank of England. They had accounts with the Bank, and kept their reserves with it, and when they ran into difficulties because of a lack of confidence as to their ability to repay depositors on demand (i.e. a run on a bank), they relied on whatever support they could get from the Bank of England.

During a crisis in 1825, many banks had to close their doors, and pressure built up in Parliament for something to be done that would enable larger and more stable banking units to be established that could more easily withstand such crises of confidence. The outcome was an Act of Parliament in 1826 (Country Bankers Act), which permitted joint stock banks to be established (and to issue their own notes), outside a radius of 65 miles of London, and at the same time the Bank of England was encouraged to open branches in the provinces. Because the new larger banks could not be established in London, which was very much the main financial and commercial centre, the 1826 Act had little effect in bringing into being the larger and more stable banking units which Parliament wanted. In consequence, the restriction on joint stock banking within London was lifted by a further Act, the Bank of England Act 1833. This permitted joint stock banking in London, provided that the banks did not issue their own notes.

By this time, the practice of paying debts by way of cheque was becoming increasingly recognised as acceptable, and in consequence the restriction in the 1833 Act concerning note issues did not have the restrictive effect that was expected. When the new banks advanced money to their customers they did so by giving them overdraft limits, or by crediting their accounts with sums transferred from loan accounts, and encouraging their customers to draw cheques to use the sums advanced. The consequence of the 1833 Act was therefore that the joint stock banks were quickly established from then on and, by a deliberate policy of buying up and absorbing the smaller banks, reduced banking in the UK to a relatively small number of large banks with networks of branches by the end of the nineteenth century.

Despite the establishment of these larger banking units, the dominance of the Bank of England, reinforced by the measure to centralise the note issue in the Bank Charter Act 1844, continued to be strengthened throughout the nineteenth and twentieth centuries by the way that the banks kept accounts with the Bank of England and settled their indebtedness with one another by drawing cheques on the central bank; and also by the fact that, because the Bank's interest rate became the leading rate of interest in the UK, the other banks related their interest rates to it. Furthermore, the importance of the Bank of England as the government's bank appreciated as new forms of government securities emerged, and the government's borrowing requirements increased enormously, especially as a consequence of the two world wars.

Because of its importance as both the bankers' bank and the government's bank, the Bank of England has ceased to compete seriously with the other banks in the provision of banking services to industry and commerce. It has some accounts for firms and individuals, but these are relatively small in number. Up to 1946 the Bank of England was privately owned but in that year it was nationalised, the shareholders being compensated with government stock. The Act nationalising the Bank gave it wide powers of control over the other banks, so that it no longer had to rely on their voluntary co-operation.

In 1979 the Bank of England's control over the other banks was tightened still further by the Banking Act of that year. This Act enforced a system by which all banks in the UK now have to be licensed by the Bank of England and the Bank has also the power to suspend or cancel a licence if it is not satisfied with the way a bank is being operated. This Act was reinforced by the Banking Act 1987 which provided for an even stricter control by the Bank. Under the European Community (EC) rules all banks within member countries must be licensed by the central bank in the country concerned and it is likely that controls over the banks will become even stricter as the EC gradually evolves.

Another provision of the 1979 Act was the establishment of a Deposit Protection Fund to which all banks must subscribe. The fund exists to protect depositors should a bank fail and in that event each depositor receives compensation to the extent of 75 per cent of his deposit with that bank up to a maximum deposit of £20,000, i.e. a maximum payment of £15,000.

Present-day functions of the Bank

The functions of the Bank of England are very similar to the functions of any central bank and, in fact, many of the central banks throughout the world were modelled on the Bank of England so that it is not surprising that their functions follow the same lines (see Figure 2.2). These are as follows:

- Operating the government's accounts
- Controlling the issue of notes and coins
- The issue and redemption of government stocks
- The Treasury bill issue
- Operating the exchange equalisation account
- Carrying out the government's monetary policy
- The Bank's international role
- Operating accounts for the banks
- Lender of last resort
- Supervising the banks

Operating the government's accounts   As the government's bank the Bank of England is responsible for running the accounts of all the government departments, which is a colossal task in view of the sheer volume and total value of transactions carried out by the government.

THE BANK OF ENGLAND

As the Government's Bank	As the Bankers' Bank
Operates Government Accounts	Keeps Accounts of The Banks
Controls the Issue of Notes	Provides Notes and Coin
and Coin	Lender of Last Resort
Issues and Redeems Government	Supervision of The Banks
Stocks	
Issues Treasury Bills	
Operates the Exchange	
Equalisation Account	
Carries Out Government's	
Monetary Policy	
The Bank's International Role	

Figure 2.2   Functions of the Bank of England

Controlling the issue of notes and coins   In conjunction with the Treasury (the government's finance department), the Bank is responsible for printing bank notes. It determines the size of the note issue, which must be increased to meet seasonal needs and in the longer term to meet the needs of an economy which, hopefully, is growing, and in which therefore the number and value of transactions is increasing. Coins are minted by the Royal Mint, which is a separate entity from the Bank of England, but it is the Bank's responsibility to ensure that adequate coins of each denomination are minted to meet the needs of the community. Similarly, it must print an appropriate quantity of each bank note and ensure that torn and dirty notes are replaced.

Issue and redemption of government stocks   The Bank is registrar for most of the government's issues of stocks. A stock is a loan to the government against which a stock certificate is issued. Each certificate indicates the name of the corporate body or individual who owns the stock and the amount that is registered in its (his) name. As registrar the Bank issues and redeems stocks, records their ownership and pays the interest when it is due. These securities represent the main part of the National Debt (i.e. the amount owed by the nation as a whole to companies, institutions and individuals in the community), and their sale and redemption provide an important means whereby the Bank of England can manipulate the amount of funds and the level of interest rates in the money market.

The Treasury bill issue   These are a special type of bill of exchange issued by the Treasury and they represent short-term loans to the government whereas government stocks are long-term loans. In the wording of the bill the Treasury undertakes to pay the face value of the bill 91 days after the date of issue. This payment is in fact the repayment of money lent to the Treasury on the day of issue plus interest at the rate determined on that day. The majority of Treasury bills are **tender** bills in that they are bid for by institutions in the money market. If an institution tenders at a price of say £97.50 (per £100) and that offer is taken up, it will in effect receive an annual rate of interest of around 10 per cent on the money because the money is being lent for approximately a quarter of a year (£2.50 × 4 per £100). The Treasury bill rate (of interest) is watched very carefully in the money market as an indicator as to how the level of interest rates generally is likely to move. The Treasury bill tender, like the issue and redemption of other government securities, is important in the context of carrying out the government's monetary policy.

Operating the exchange equalisation account   By operating this account the Bank is able to influence the value of sterling and other currencies in the foreign exchange market.

The account holds all of the UK reserves of gold and foreign currencies. When sterling is weak (i.e. it has become less valuable in terms of other currencies in the foreign exchange market), the Bank of England will sell some foreign currency, maybe US dollars, in exchange for sterling. This reduces the supply of sterling in the foreign exchange market and increases the supply of the foreign currency; this tends to increase the value of sterling and to reduce the value of the foreign currency and to bring about a state of equilibrium in the market. When sterling is particularly strong the bank must operate the account in the opposite direction – sell sterling in exchange for dollars – in order to keep down the value of the pound and to increase the value of the dollar.

Carrying out the government's monetary policy   It is vital that the government controls the total of the money supply if it is to succeed in maintaining constant, or fairly constant, prices: in other words if it is to avoid inflation. As we saw in Chapter 1, the majority of the money supply, whichever way it is measured, is made up of bank deposits, and therefore any attempt to control the money supply must involve influencing or determining the size of bank deposits. The main determinants of the size of deposits are the level of interest rates and sale and purchase of government securities, which are both within the control of the Bank of England, though ultimately it is the government which dictates how the Bank, as its agent, must use these devices.

The Bank's international role   The Governor of the Bank of England is responsible not only for carrying out the government's monetary policy, but also for meeting with other central bank governors to discuss international monetary problems, and to decide upon joint action to deal with them.

Accounts of the banks   Each of the other British banks keeps accounts with the Bank of England, and through these they are able to settle transactions with one another, i.e. to draw cheques on the Bank.

The Bank of England maintains accounts for overseas banks as well as the British banks, and these include the central banks' accounts through which it is possible to carry out transactions relating to loans between countries and through such institutions as the International Monetary Fund (IMF). The Bank of England also holds accounts for the IMF and other international institutions.

The balances of the British banks' accounts with the Bank of England form part of their cash reserves in that they can draw upon them at any time, and they are maintained at the minimum amount it is reckoned they need for the day-to-day transactions that are settled through the accounts.

Lender of last resort   It is vital that a central bank should act as lender of last resort to the banking system. If the banks are short of funds and are unable to acquire additional funds from other sources, then they must have the support of the central bank, but the central bank is able to determine the price that has to be paid for that support, i.e. the rate of interest charged. In the UK, the Bank of England gives this support indirectly in that it is the London discount houses and not the banks that are forced to obtain funds from the Bank of England if they are short. If the supply of funds in the London money market is insufficient, then the banks call in some of the 'call money' from the discount houses, forcing them to seek assistance. This assistance may be given by the Bank directly buying bills or, alternatively, the Bank may choose to give indirect assistance by buying bills from the banks, enabling them to restore their call money loans to the discount houses or, rarely these days, lending to them. Acting as lender of last resort provides the central bank with a weapon to use as part of the government's monetary policy.

Supervision of the banks   Under the Banking Acts 1979 and 1987 the Bank of England is able to demand very detailed statistical returns from the other banks in order to ensure that the banks are being operated on safe and prudential lines. If the Bank is not satisfied with a particular bank's returns it is able to insist that measures are taken to put matters right. For instance, the Bank might insist that the offending bank build up its liquid assets and run down its holdings of longer-term assets in order to maintain a more satisfactory liquidity ratio. If a bank fails to follow the guidelines given by the Bank of England the ultimate sanction of withdrawing that bank's licence to accept deposits could be used (see p. 22).

2.3   The Retail Banks

Origins of the banks

In looking at the relationship between the Bank of England and the other banks, we touched upon the origins and development of the banks. The larger present-day banks, i.e. Barclays, Lloyds, Midland and National Westminster, can trace their origins to the developments following the 1833 Banking Act which permitted the establishment of joint stock banks. The first of these banks was the National County and Westminster in 1835 and it was quickly followed by the other three plus the National Provincial Bank which merged with Westminster

Bank much later (in 1968) to form NatWest. These joint stock banks quickly grew during the second half of the nineteenth century, mostly by absorbing the hundreds of small private banks. The amalgamation process continued, but at a much slower pace, into the twentieth century, so that there are now relatively few banks and, apart from the merchant banks and foreign banks which we will look at later, they all have networks of branches.

The term **retail banks** is used to include all of the banks which have branch networks through which they are able to offer a wide range of services over the counter to a large number of customers. Sometimes the term **high street banks** is used to mean the same thing, and on occasions the term **commercial banks** is used, though less commonly these days.

The retail banks now comprise the following:

- **Barclays**
- **Lloyds**
- **Midland** (now owned by the Hongkong and Shanghai Bank)
- **National Westminster** (including Coutts)
- **TSB Bank**
- **Abbey National**
- **Allied Irish Banks**
- **Co-operative Bank**
- **Yorkshire Bank**
- **Bank of Scotland**
- **Clydesdale Bank**
- **Royal Bank of Scotland**
- **Girobank**
- **Ulster Bank**
- **Bank of Ireland**
- **Northern Bank**

Of these Barclays, Lloyds, Midland and National Westminster are the biggest, closely followed by TSB and Abbey National. The TSB bank was created in 1985 as a result of the Trustee Savings Bank Act 1976 which permitted the amalgamation of the then existing 72 Trustee Savings Banks into one large banking group, the TSB Group. At one time (in 1819) there were 465 small individual trustee savings banks serving local communities. As the name suggests, they were simply savings banks that looked after their customers' deposits. They paid interest on these deposits and trustees invested them with the National Debt Commissioners. The Abbey National is technically a bank because when it became a public limited company in 1989 it automatically came under the Banking Act 1987 instead of the Building Societies Act 1986; however, it still functions very much as a building society, though like all building societies it offers some services which are very much akin to those offered by the banks, as we shall see later. The Girobank was established as the National Giro in 1968 by the government as a service to be operated and owned by the Post Office and to enable depositors to send requests for funds to be transferred to third parties through the post to the bank's computer centre at Bootle. It was reorganised in 1978 and renamed the National Girobank providing cheque books and credit facilities to its customers for the first time. It was subsequently floated as a public company, Girobank plc, and purchased by the Alliance and Leicester Building Society.

The most important services which the retail banks provide are:

- The acceptance of deposits
- The provision of ways in which deposits can be transferred
- The provision of credit

Let us look briefly at each one of these services in turn.

Acceptance of deposits   This simply means that a bank must be prepared to take deposits of cash and cheques from its customers and to credit their accounts with them. The bank keeps these funds for their customers and undertakes to repay them on demand if the money is on a current account, or at the expiry of a period of notice if the money is on an investment account (see p. 122).

The provision of ways in which deposits can be transferred   Money on current account can be withdrawn by presenting a cheque for cash at the bank's counter or issuing it to a third party who can then pay it into his bank account or cash it at the counter if it is an open (an uncrossed) cheque. The vast majority of third party cheques are in fact crossed and are presented through the banks' clearing system to the banks on which they are drawn. Alternatively the customer may draw on his deposit through an ATM; he may authorise the bank to make payments from the account on his behalf against a standing order or a direct debit; or he may use his switch or Delta card.

The provision of credit   This means that the banks must be prepared to lend money to their customers. This does not mean that every customer is **entitled** to borrow, far from it, but that the banks are willing to provide loans to those customers who are sufficiently creditworthy. This means that their assets and income must be such that they are able to repay the advance over the time period that is agreed at the outset, and also to pay the interest as it falls due. Lending money in this way is the main source of income to the banks – they accept deposits and pay modest rates of interest, if any, on them, and then lend most of their deposits at rates of interest that are considerably higher than those paid on deposits.

These are by no means all the services that the retail banks offer their customers, and indeed they offer a wide range of services and, mostly through subsidiary companies, they offer services (products) that compete with those offered by the merchant banks and by many of the financial intermediaries we shall be examining in Chapter 3 such as building societies, insurance companies, and unit trusts.

Savings banks come into a separate category because they offer only the first two of the three main services we looked at above, and even as far as the means whereby deposits can be transferred is concerned, cheque books are not provided and cheques or warrants must be requested if the depositor wishes to make a payment to a third party. The best example of a savings bank is the National Savings Bank which is operated over post office counters but is in fact run by a government department, the Department of National Savings. It started off in 1861 as the Post Office Savings Bank but was renamed in 1971. We shall look at the National Savings Bank in detail in Chapter 3.

You will appreciate that central banks are also in a separate category in that they do not normally offer banking services to members of the public, concentrating instead on the requirements of the government sector and in offering services to the banks.

2.4   The Wholesale Banks

This term is applied to those banks which in the main buy deposits from the money market and then relend them at higher rates of interest either to their business customers or to other institutions in the money market. This term is a little misleading in that most banks, including the retail banks, are engaged in the wholesale market, but whereas the retail banks have networks of branches through which to accept deposits from their millions of customers, the wholesale banks do not usually have any branches, or if they do they are limited to just a small number.

Examples of wholesale banks are the merchant banks, the discount houses and, to some extent, the overseas banks in the UK. We shall examine the functions of the discount houses and the overseas banks later in the chapter, but first let us look at the merchant banks and contrast them with the retail banks.

2.5   The Merchant Banks

Origin of the banks

The merchant banks originated as institutions which accepted bills of exchange on behalf of their customers, i.e. they undertook to pay the bills by writing 'accepted' across the face of the bills and adding their signature. The bankers were themselves wealthy merchants of international repute, and so highly respected and trusted that if they could be persuaded to add their names to bills of exchange these bills became readily discountable in the London discount market at the lowest rate of interest. As we have seen, by accepting a bill of exchange, the acceptor undertakes to pay it at maturity, and no banker is going to undertake such a task on behalf of a customer unless he is really sure of his creditworthiness. Like a bank gold card, such an acceptance says quite a lot about the person or firm concerned!

The merchant bank's willingness to accept bills on behalf of the customer (a British importer, maybe) was often signified in the form of a letter, and this was the origin of the **acceptance credit**, the issue of which is a major activity of most of the merchant banks. The bank lends its name, but not necessarily its money, to the customer. It trusts that by the time the bills which have been accepted are presented for payment, there will be sufficient funds in the customer's account to meet them, and hence no borrowing will be involved. The customer will have been able to borrow, however, by discounting the bill with a London discount house (see below), and it is the discounter of the bill that in effect lends the money to him until the date of maturity.

The merchant bank charges a commission for opening an acceptance credit, and for accepting bills, and makes a profit from such commission rather than from interest on lending to the importer. This is not to say that the merchant banks do not lend money – they certainly do, as we shall see later – but traditionally their function has not been to accept deposits from customers and use the funds to lend by way of loans and overdrafts.

The wealthy merchant banker found that his activities as an acceptor of bills were lucrative, and dropped his trading activities in favour of the acceptance business. The merchant banks became known as acceptance houses and today they include such well-known names as Baring Bros, Lazards, and Rothschilds. They are not the only banks that accept bills of exchange, of course (most banks offer this facility), but acceptances account for a much greater part of a merchant bank's activities than is the case with the retail banks.

Present-day functions

The merchant banks have moved a long way from being primarily accepting houses, and the distinction between retail banking and merchant banking has become far less clear in that the retail banks now have merchant bank subsidiaries and the merchant banks have taken on much more ordinary retail banking business, and have been much more prepared to accept deposits and to provide loans and overdrafts. Their main present-day functions can be summarised as follows:

- Services to importers and exporters
- Issuing shares and advising companies
- Activities in the money markets and commodity markets
- Managing investment portfolios
- Factoring and leasing

Services to importers and exporters   In addition to the acceptance of bills of exchange already referred to, the merchant banks provide a wide range of services to facilitate the import and export of goods, including documentary credits, accepting and collecting documentary bills, and foreign exchange requirements.

Issuing shares and advising companies   As issuing houses the merchant banks have been traditionally responsible for advising and assisting corporate bodies in the issue of shares; helping partnerships and private companies 'go public', i.e. to issue shares as public companies; and helping public companies in obtaining additional capital by issuing new shares and debentures. They are very much involved in takeovers and mergers, steering through the very delicate and intricate negotiations that these involve.

Activities in the money markets and commodity markets   These include borrowing and lending on a wholesale basis in the money markets, including the Eurocurrency market, issuing and dealing in certificates of deposit, foreign exchange dealing and dealing in the commodity markets in gold and silver bullion and other commodities.

Managing investment portfolios   Where a customer, whether a private individual or a corporate body, has funds to invest, a merchant bank will be prepared to carry out investments in stocks and shares on behalf of the customer and monitor them, and advise and carry out changes in the holdings either on its own initiative or in consultation with the customer.

Factoring and leasing   Factoring involves the purchase of a trader's invoices at their face value less discount and usually, though not always, on a non-recourse basis, so that the loss if the purchaser does not pay up is borne by the factor. To the seller the big advantage of factoring his debts is that he is virtually trading entirely for cash and will have no debtors in his balance sheet other than the factoring house. The factoring house may be willing to pay immediately a large proportion of the cash that is due, which is tantamount to an advance because it may take some time to obtain payment from the buyers. This fact is taken into account in the discount that is charged when the invoices are purchased.

Leasing involves purchasing the machinery or equipment that the bank's customer needs and then leasing it to him. The asset remains the property of the bank or leasing company, but it may ultimately be sold to the customer at a knockdown price after it has been leased for a long period. The advantage to the bank's customer is that he does not need to borrow the necessary capital to buy the asset and will know at the outset how much to allow in his cost of production figures for the rental of the machinery. There is no need either to allow for depreciation of the asset because that is the responsibility of the owners (the bank).

It must not be assumed that the merchant banks are the only institutions that carry out these services and, as has been pointed out, the retail banks have a big stake in all of them.

2.6   The Discount Houses

In looking at the functions of the Bank of England in Section 2.2 above, we came across the discount houses as the institutions through which the Bank acts as lender of last resort. We need now to look at the functions of the discount houses, (which comprise the London Discount Market), in greater detail.

The London discount market consists of nine discount houses (which are recognised banks under the Banking Acts 1979 and 1987), examples of which are Cater Allen, Union Discount, and Gerrard and National, plus a number of smaller houses that specialise in particular fields such as dealing in bullion or as stock dealers. The discount houses have the privilege of being able to borrow from the Bank of England as lender of last resort.

The discount houses originated as institutions that would discount commercial bills of exchange, i.e. they would buy bills of exchange for their face value less discount. The discount represented a rate of interest charged for paying over money which was not going to be recouped until the bill matured and was presented for payment. Before a discount house would discount a bill, it would have to be satisfied with the reputation of the parties concerned with it, i.e. the drawer (and, more especially, the drawee and acceptor – see p. 89 for definitions of these terms). It will be appreciated that the discount house relies on the integrity of the person who is expected to pay the bill at its maturity.

Through the discounting of bills the discount houses provided a vital service in the UK prior to the establishment of the network of branch banks in the latter part of the nineteenth century. They facilitated the movement of funds by discounting for industrialists and merchants bills which they resold to the banks that were looking for ways of investing surplus funds. Once the banks took over the role of transferring funds by accepting deposits of the wealthy through their branch networks and lending them to those in need of working capital, i.e. acting as financial intermediaries on a big scale, the need for domestic bills of exchange diminished. Similarly the increased use of cheques as a means of payment also reduced the reliance on bills of exchange for this purpose. Instead the discount houses concentrated more on the discounting of bills drawn in connection with overseas trade and this is still an important activity. In addition, from 1914, the government has issued Treasury bills as a means of obtaining short-term finance, and the discount houses have invested large sums of borrowed money in these bills as well as in government stocks. They buy bills, stocks, and certificates of deposit and resell them to the banks and other institutions in the money markets, making a small turn (profit) on them as they do so.

In order to buy the securities, the discount houses borrow wholesale from the banks and other financial intermediaries and do not have retail branches. Much of this borrowing is on a short-term basis, overnight or for a maximum of 14 days, and if any of this is called in it may cause the discount houses to become short of funds. It is then that the Bank of England acts as lender of last resort as we saw on p. 25, and this is one way in which it can influence the movement of interest rates up or down in order to carry out the government's monetary policy.

2.7   Foreign Banks

London has always been a major financial centre of the world, and as such has attracted overseas banks. These banks have seen the need either to open offices in

London at which to station representatives, or to open branches at which full banking services are offered. There has been a rapid increase in the number of foreign banks in London since the 1950s, attracted by the existence and development of Euro-currency markets, the establishment and expansion of the EC, North Sea oil, and by the needs of immigrants into the UK. Japanese and US business corporations and banks have been especially active in establishing themselves in Europe, particularly since the EC was established.

The amount of deposits held by the several hundred foreign banks in London, especially those denominated in foreign currency, is enormous and thus these banks play a very important part in the London Money Market. Some of the banks take in retail deposits, mostly from immigrants, but in the main their deposits are wholesale deposits which are borrowed and lent in the money markets. To some extent they lend to their retail customers, especially to businesses.

Review Questions

1   When was the Bank of England established, and what advantages did it have from the outset compared with the other banks? (2.2)

2   Why did the other banks become very dependent upon the Bank of England? (2.2)

3   What was the purpose of the Country Bankers Act 1826 and the Bank of England Act 1833? (2.2)

4   What were the consequences of the 1833 Act? (2.2)

5   Does the Bank of England compete with the other banks in the provision of services to industry and commerce? (2.2)

6   When, and how, was the Bank of England nationalised? (2.2)

7   What were the effects of the 1979 and 1987 Banking Acts? (2.2)

8   What is meant by the term 'the government's bank'? (2.2)

9   Which body is responsible for minting coins? (2.2)

10   Is the Bank of England responsible for the note issue? (2.2)

11   What is meant by the the issue and redemption of government stocks? (2.2)

12   What is a Treasury bill, and how is the rate of interest on it calculated? (2.2)

13   How does the exchange equalisation account operate? (2.2)

14   Which institution is responsible for carrying out the government's monetary policy? (2.2)

15   What is the Bank of England's international role? (2.2)

16   Why do the banks keep accounts with the Bank of England? (2.2)

17   Explain the Bank of England's role as lender of last resort. (2.2)

18   How does the Bank of England supervise the banks? (2.2)

19   Explain what is meant by a retail bank. (2.3)

20   Prepare a list of the retail banks. (2.3)

21   Which are the three main functions of a retail bank? (2.3)

Review Questions cont'd.

22 What is meant by wholesale banking? (2.4)
23 Distinguish between a retail bank and a merchant bank (2.5)
24 How did the merchant banks originate? (2.5)
25 What are the main services of a merchant bank? (2.5)
26 Explain how the discount houses originated. (2.6)
27 Which institutions are given the privilege of being able to borrow from the Bank of England as lender of last resort? (2.6)
28 Are the foreign banks in London retail banks or wholesale banks? (2.7)

Past Examination Questions

1 Make brief notes on the *main* roles of:
   (i)   the Bank of England
   (ii) merchant banks.   (Part question, *10 marks*)

2 State which institutions carry out each of the following roles. Outline their main functions or activities in each case:
   (i)   Controls, monitors and advises the banking system.   (*10 marks*)

   (ii) Provides finance and advice to companies, arranges for flotations and deals in financial markets.   (*5 marks*)

   (iii) Set up originally to provide a simple money transmission service and has now extended its activities into the use of current account banking to the lower income groups and the provision of a wide range of services through the Post Office.   (*5 marks*)

3 Define 'financial intermediation', and explain the advantages associated with the practice.   (Part question, *12 marks*)

3 Other financial intermediaries and products

┌─ **Chapter objectives** ───

When you have carefully studied this chapter you should be able to:
- Explain the role of the building societies
- Distinguish between the two types of account run by the National Savings Bank and describe each of the National Savings products
- Comment on the activities of the finance houses
- Explain the functions and products of the insurance companies and the role of Lloyds of London
- Define a unit trust in detail and distinguish it from an investment trust
- Explain the functions of a friendly society and a credit union
- Define the purpose and functions of the London Stock Exchange
- Explain what is meant by the London Money Market

3.1 Introduction

In Chapter 2 we examined the roles of the various types of banks, and we now need to look at the other financial intermediaries and their products in some detail. In doing so, we must bear in mind that the banks offer financial products in competition with them so that when we examine the advantages of an invest- ment in a unit trust, for instance, we are looking at the advantages of a service which a large retail bank may offer through a subsidiary company. The banks are also active on the Stock Exchange through their acquisitions of stockbroker and market maker companies. We shall examine the services of the banks in detail in Chapters 8 and 9.

3.2 Building Societies

Apart from the Abbey National, which became a public company in 1989, the building societies are owned by their customers who have deposited money in share accounts and who receive interest and not dividends on their investment.

There are still some deposit account holders who technically (because they are not shareholders) do not participate in affairs of the society, and in the event of liquidation they would be treated as creditors and be given preferential treatment over shareholders. However, the majority of accounts are share accounts.

In the last 20 years the building societies have been the banks' main competitor for personal deposits. For many years they had the privilege of paying interest on deposit and share accounts net of income tax and they opened for longer hours than the banks, and thus were able to attract customers away from the banks. However, since 1985 the banks have been placed on the same footing as far as paying interest net of tax is concerned and they have kept their branches open for longer hours and, in many cases, on Saturday mornings. Several of the societies now offer current account facilities, including cheque books, in competition with the banks and have become members of APACS (see p. 117) in order to avail themselves of clearing facilities, especially the electronic facilities of BACS. The societies pay interest on their current accounts, such as Nationwide's Flexi Account, and this competition forced the banks to do the same from 1988. The building societies established ATM networks which eventually merged as one network, Link, which now competes with the two networks run by the banks. A number of the societies have established homebanking facilities whereby customers can make enquiries about the balances on their accounts and recent transactions on them, order cheque books, paying-in books and statements, arrange standing orders, transfer funds from one account to another and pay household bills with some suppliers directly.

The supervision of the building societies is carried out by the Chief Registrar of Friendly Societies, and their range of activities is limited, but the Building Societies Act 1986 permitted them to lend for purposes other than house purchase to a limited extent and to become involved in running estate agencies and even in building houses. The Abbey National, as a public company, comes under the Banking Acts 1979 and 1987, and is therefore under the supervision of the Bank of England.

Building societies accept their shareholders' savings mostly on a short-term basis and the rate of interest paid varies with the amount invested and the length of notice that is required. On interest-bearing current accounts the interest is quite low, especially on small amounts, and one society pays no interest at all on balances below £100. On share accounts somewhat higher rates are paid where there is instant access, whilst on investment accounts involving 3 months' or even 6 months' notice for withdrawal, interest rates are some 3 or 4 per cent higher than the basic rate on instant access accounts. Several of the societies offer postal accounts on which they offer better rates of interest, even on instant access, because the amount of work involved is minimised. The Finance Act 1983 gave the societies power to raise money through the wholesale money markets by the use of certificates of deposit, and hence they now compete with the banks for these funds.

The main way in which the building societies invest their shareholders' funds is of course by lending on a long-term basis against mortgages on house property. Mortgages are for varying periods of years, but the most usual is 25 years. Here again there has been great competition between the banks and the building societies in recent years. During the 1980s the banks lent enormous sums by way of mortgages, and the amount of mortgage finance outstanding in the books of the largest of the banks is not far short of the total of the largest of the building societies.

To sum up, the building societies provide the following services:

- Types of account   Share accounts (subject to various periods of notice and rates of interest)
  Deposit accounts
  Postal accounts
  TESSA accounts
  Current accounts
- Methods of payment   Cheques and cheque guarantee cards
  Switch and Delta cards
  Homebanking
  Standing orders and direct debits
  ATMs
- Types of loans   Mortgages
  House improvement loans
  Personal loans

3.3   Insurance Companies

Very substantial sums of money are collected by the insurance companies each year from policy holders and investors in their various schemes, and their funds are employed mostly on a long-term basis – especially the life assurance funds, repayment of which will be spread over the years ahead. The very size of their investments makes the insurance companies very active and important in the money markets. Strictly speaking the term **insurance** is applied to cover for the risks that apply to goods and property, such as house insurance and car insurance, and the term **assurance** applies to insurance of the person, e.g. life assurance, endowment assurance, pension schemes (see Figure 3.1). However, the word insurance is commonly used to mean all types of cover, and the companies concerned are generally referred to as insurance companies.

Most of the insurance companies are public limited companies (plcs) and are quoted on the Stock Exchange, but there are some mutual companies that are owned by their policy holders. Lloyds of London is where policies are underwritten by a large group of individuals, many of whom have suffered the loss of all their subscribed capital in recent years as the result of disasters such as the gale damage in 1987, oil slicks, flooding and earthquakes, and disasters at sea and in the air.

All insurance companies offer most of the range of insurance cover available and this includes life assurance, pension plans and annuities.

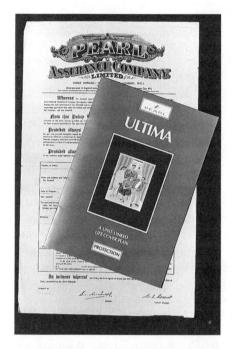

Insurance (Things)	Assurance (Persons)
	Life Policies
Houses and Contents	Endowment Policies
Cars	Mortgage Protection
Motor Cycles	Policies
Ships	Pension Schemes
Aircraft	Annuities

Figure 3.1   Insurance and assurance

Life assurance

The two main types of life cover are **whole life** and **endowment** assurance. Whole life assurance covers the policy holder right up to the date of his death. He pays premiums during the whole of his lifetime, or possibly for a set period of years, and the assurance company pays out the principal sum plus, possibly, some declared bonuses, into his estate or to a named person upon his death. This obviously benefits those who inherit and not the policy holder. Endowment cover is for a set period of years or upon the death of the policy holder should he die during that period. The cover can be either with profits or without. The former is more expensive than the latter (i.e. the premiums are higher) because the policy holder shares in the profits made by the company and accrued profits are paid out in addition to the principal sum upon maturity of the policy.

A variation of whole life cover is the **term assurance** policy where the policy holder is assured against his death for a set period of time and if he survives that period the insurance company pays out nothing. Other risks that can be insured against on the same basis are unemployment and protracted illness or disability. Good examples of term policies are the **mortgage protection** policy and the **unemployment protection** policy. These policies protect the policy holder (and the bank or building society that has lent his money) against his death (or unemployment) during the term of the policy. Because if he survives, or is not unemployed, the insurance company has nothing to pay out, the premiums on this type of policy are very much lower than those for whole life or endowment.

Pension plans

The life assurance companies are also very much involved in the provision of pension schemes, both group schemes for companies, and private pension schemes for individuals. Whilst many large employers run their own pension scheme, other companies, especially the smaller ones, prefer to pass the job on to an assurance company. The employer pays in monthly contributions from employees and from the company on behalf of the employees, and as each employee retires he is entitled to a pension which is usually based on his salary or wages at the time of retirement. Quite often the employee has the option of taking a lump sum and a smaller pension and may also be able to set aside some of his pension in order that his wife should receive a pension should he die before her. Should an employee resign his job he is given the option of either leaving his contributions in the scheme and receiving a frozen pension when he reaches retirement age based on the amount of these contributions, or transferring a lump sum from the pension fund to a new pension scheme, either that of his new employer or a private pension scheme of his own.

Annuities

In order to boost his or her income an individual with a sizeable amount of capital to invest could take out an annuity with an assurance company. A lump sum payment will provide the annuitant with a regular income of a fixed amount or, possibly, an amount which increases by an agreed percentage each year to allow for inflation, and these payments go on until date of death. A husband and wife may take out a joint annuity which ensures that should one of them die the partner will continue to receive the payments until he or she dies.

The main point about an annuity is that the capital sum becomes the property of the assurance company – the annuity dies with the annuitant. The amount of the annuity payments will therefore be based on the expectation of life of the annuitant and the younger he is at the time that the annuity is taken out the lower will be the annuity payments, because the assurance company can expect that by the law of averages it will be paying out for a longer period of time. For an old person, especially one with no family, an annuity is likely to produce a much better return than most other forms of investment and with some exemption from income tax, but the capital invested will be lost to his or her estate. There are some types of annuity which provide for a return of some of the capital sum invested should the annuitant die within a prescribed short period of time after taking out the annuity.

A deferred annuity is one which does not commence until the annuitant reaches a particular age (maybe retirement age) and the assurance company will have the use of the capital sum until that time is reached. Because of this the amount it is willing to pay as an annuity is higher than it would otherwise be.

3.4   Finance Houses

At one time hire purchase finance was the principal form of finance provided by the finance houses, but they have since widened the scope of their activities very considerably and now also offer straightforward loans to personal borrows, both secured and unsecured. To industry and commerce they now provide loans as well as factoring and leasing services.

Hire-purchase finance involves an agreement between the person who buys the goods (e.g. a car or a washing machine) that the finance house will pay for them, apart from an initial deposit, and then the buyer repays over two or three years in regular monthly instalments which include interest as well as principal. The rate of interest is high compared with the rate on straightforward bank overdrafts because it is charged on the full amount lent for the whole period of the loan, despite the fact that the amount of the loan is gradually reduced, and on average over the whole period is only about half the size of the original amount. Another factor determining the rate of interest is the risk of non-payment. Technically the goods remain the property of the hire purchase company until the loan is completely repaid and the company has the right to repossess the goods.

To a considerable extent the finance houses have become involved in making personal loans, both secured and unsecured. Many of the loans have been against a second mortgage on the customer's house.

In addition to providing finance to the individual to buy a car, the finance houses also provide finance for the car dealer to bridge the period between the time when the car is purchased from the manufacturer and the time that it is sold. The finance houses also lend to other small and medium-sized companies, mostly to enable them to buy machinery and equipment.

Factoring involves buying the seller's invoices for their face value less discount and then pursuing the purchaser for the money. Leasing involves buying the machinery or equipment for the customer and then renting it to him.

The majority of finance houses are now owned by the banks, so that where an application for an advance is unsuitable for the type of finance that the bank provides, it may well pass the request on to its subsidiary finance house. The finance houses attract deposits from the general public by paying high rates of interest and they also borrow in the wholesale money market.

3.5   Unit Trusts

A unit trust collects together the savings of a large number of subscribers and invests these funds in stocks and shares on behalf of them jointly. Each subscriber's capital is spread over a wide range of industrial and/or government investments in a way that would be impossible if he or she were directly to invest any modest funds.

The investor is allocated units according to the amount of the subscription, and the daily valuation of units is calculated and published on the basis of the total worth of the trust funds divided by the number of units issued. Investors may subscribe to the fund for blocks of units or, in many cases, agree to subscribe a regular sum each month. The income of the unit trust is distributed to the unit holders in either of two ways – either by half-yearly payments to their bank accounts (income units) or by increasing the holders' unit holdings (accumulation units). If the unit holder wants a regular income he will obviously choose a unit trust fund that provides for the former, whilst someone who is looking for capital growth will choose a unit trust which distributes the income as additional units.

A unit trust is not a company and has no share capital of its own. The managers, however, are separate companies who charge a management fee for the day-to-day running of the trust with an obligation to invest the unit holders' funds as wisely as possible in order to produce a good return and capital growth. The trustees are in the main banks and insurance companies. Some of the large retail banks now run their own unit trusts through subsidiary or associated companies and derive an income from the management charges.

Since the later 1980s it has been possible for holders of Personal Equity Plans (PEPs) to hold investments in unit trusts within their plans up to certain limits and PEPs which include unit trusts have become very popular. PEPs were introduced by the government to encourage wider share ownership. Taxpayers who have such a plan with one of the financial intermediaries can claim tax exemption on the dividends and capital gains in respect of the shares that are held within the plan.

Unit trusts specialise in particular types of investments and the name of each trust will indicate this specialisation. For instance, the trust might be called European Income and this signifies that its funds are invested in shares in European companies that produce good dividends to be distributed as income, whereas another may be called Japanese Growth and specialise in investing in Japanese companies whose shares are likely to appreciate in value but not necessarily produce high income. The improved value of these shares will be reflected in the total value of the fund and hence the value of the units, i.e. the fund will have produced capital growth for the unit holders.

The unit holder is able to redeem his units by selling them to the unit trust managers at the price quoted for the particular units on the day of the transaction. Prices are published in the press each weekday and for each unit trust there are two prices. One is the bid price and the other is the offer price: the bid price is higher than the offer price and is the amount at which the trust managers are willing to sell units, the offer price is the price at which they are willing to buy units.

To sum up, unit trusts offer the following services and advantages:

- Types of trust Accumulation units or income units
  Lump sum or regular payments
  General or specialised
- Advantages Investor can spread the risk over number of industries/countries
  Units easily bought and sold and valued
  Can be part of PEP
  Specialised managers

3.6 Investment Trusts

Investment trusts are limited companies which buy stocks and shares with the capital invested by their proprietors. The investment trust's shares are quoted on the Stock Exchange and thus the shareholders may redeem their capital by selling their shares on the market (and not by selling them to the trust itself, as is the case with unit trusts). The trusts sometimes raise additional funds by issuing loan stocks, and these funds are invested in stocks and shares. The income from the trust's holdings of stocks and shares is used to pay interest on loan stock and dividends to the shareholders. The value of the trust's own shares is determined in the market by the forces of supply and demand.

Whereas investments in unit trusts tend to be relatively small and may be by regular monthly subscription, investments in investment trusts tend to be larger and are not on a regular basis. The investor in stocks and shares generally may choose to put some of his capital into investment trust shares because the price and/or the yield is particularly attractive compared with that of shares in other sectors. He buys and sells through a stockbroker in just the same way as he would do for other shares and has to pay the normal commission for the service, which tends to be particularly high pro rata for buying and selling small amounts of shares.

3.7   Friendly Societies

Friendly societies originated as small local societies that protected working class people when they were retired, unemployed or ill, and provided some help to widows and orphans. Members paid small weekly contributions which enabled them to seek help when they needed it. They were, and still are, mutual societies owned by their members, with paid officials to run them. They come under the control of the Registrar of Friendly Societies.

The societies have developed into just a few large organisations whose role is to provide savings schemes which are free of tax, and because of this, the amounts that can be invested in them are strictly limited.

The savings **plans** are tied up with endowment assurance policies and run for 10 years, though they may be surrendered earlier. During that time the investor's funds are employed half in company shares and the rest in government stocks, building societies and other safe investments. The maximum investment is £18 per month or £200 per year and lump sum investments up to £1600.

Funds may also be invested in savings **bonds** with a minimum of £1,000. The investment period varies, with a minimum of 5 years and a regular monthly income may be taken. As with savings plans, neither income tax nor capital gains tax are payable.

Friendly societies are now permitted to run PEPs and unit trusts and to provide insurance and pension fund services.

3.8   Credit Unions

Credit unions are cooperative organisations controlled by the Credit Union Act 1979, and supervised by the Registrar of Friendly Societies. Their role is to provide an avenue for savings by the members and to supply them with cheap credit. Many of the unions are associated with the Church and it is one of the aims that they should be very much involved in local communities. The rate of interest on deposits is paid gross but it is quite low. All deposits are guaranteed against loss. Members may borrow at a relatively low fixed rate up to a maximum of £5,000 (which can be increased if the member has a savings account with the union).

3.9   National Savings Products

The government encourages personal saving by offering various forms of investment through the Department of National Savings which uses the Post Office
retail counters and the postal service in order to obtain subscriptions and to repay
deposits and redeem maturing or surrendered assets (see Figure 3.2).

National Savings Bank

We have looked very briefly at the National Savings Bank in Chapter 2 (see
p. 28) but we now need to examine its services in more detail.

The National Savings Bank provides in the main outlets for savings and does
not provide cheque books and other means of transferring funds in the way that
the retail banks do. Nor does it provide loans and overdrafts. The bank offers two
types of accounts, ordinary accounts and investment accounts.

Ordinary accounts   These are designed for small savings and an account can be
opened with as little as £10. The standard rate of interest at the time of writing is
2.5 per cent, but for the depositor who keeps his or her account opened for at
least 1 calender year (from January to December) and maintains a minimum balance of £500 the rate goes up to 3.75 per cent. The maximum balance permitted
is £10,000. No income tax is payable on the first £70 per annum of interest.

Normally withdrawals on demand (at any post office) are limited to £100 and
the bank book is retained for checking if the demand exceeds £50, and larger
amounts may be withdrawn in a few days by submitting a form to National Savings at Glasgow – this can be by crossed warrant or in cash at a named post
office. However, 'Regular Customers', i.e. those who have used an Ordinary
Account at a chosen post office for at least 6 months, may draw up to £250 in
cash at that post office and the bank book is not retained.

The rate of interest is very low and withdrawal facilities are limited and the
pass book may be retained, but against these disadvantages are the advantages of
having a large number of outlets and a bank that is backed by the government.

Investment accounts   These accounts attract a higher rate of interest (at the time
of writing 6.25 per cent) and it is paid gross, but withdrawals are subject to 1
month's notice. The minimum deposit is £5 and the maximum £25,000. The
interest is credited gross on 31 December each year and it is not necessary for an
Inland Revenue registration form to be completed in order to obtain the interest
gross, as it is for banks and building societies.

Savings certificates   These used to be known as national savings certificates.
There are two types of savings certificate, the ordinary issue and the index-linked
issue. The former attract a fixed rate of growth over their 5 year life whilst the
latter attract interest equal to the annual rate of inflation (based on the Index of

Figure 3.2   National Savings products

Retail Prices, RPI) plus 3.25 per cent. All interest is free of income tax and capital gains tax. The maximum investment is £10,000 for each issue. For both types of certificate the rate of interest builds up during the life of the certificate – for instance, the 6th Index-linked issue attracts interest as follows:

- Year 1   RPI + 1.5 per cent
- Year 2   RPI + 2.0 per cent
- Year 3   RPI + 2.75 per cent
- Year 4   RPI + 3.75 per cent from date of purchase
- Year 5   RPI + 6.32 per cent from date of purchase

These rates average out to RPI plus 3.25 per cent compound.

Yearly plan

This is a way of saving monthly to build up a capital sum at a rate of return which is guaranteed for 5 years and which is free from income tax and capital gains tax. The investor undertakes to save a monthly sum of between £20 and £400 for a period of a year by standing order. He is issued with a Yearly Plan Certificate. If at the end of the first year he carries on for a further 4 years he achieves the maximum return which, at the time of writing, is 5.75 per cent per annum. Each year an additional Yearly Plan may be taken out each with its own 5-year rate of return.

Income bonds

These provide for a regular monthly income paid gross in return for a lump sum investment. The minimum purchase is £2,000 and the maximum £250,000. In July 1993 the rate of interest was 7 per cent per annum, producing a gross annual income of £3,500 on an investment of £50,000.

All or part of a bond may be encashed subject to 3 months' notice and if this is during the first year of the bond interest is reduced by 50 per cent.

First option bonds

These are more flexible than income bonds but they do not provide a monthly income – interest is payable on the anniversary date each year. FIRST stands for Fixed Interest Rate Savings Tax-paid, and it is an option bond because at the end of each year the investor has the option of carrying on for another 12 months at the then fixed rate or cashing in the bond. In July 1993 the rate of interest was 6.34 per cent gross and from this tax is deducted at the standard rate before payment, i.e. the net payment is 4.75 per cent. If a bond is for £20,000 or more it attracts a bonus of 0.4 per cent gross.

No interest is paid on repayments before the first anniversary date, and between subsequent anniversary dates it is reduced by 50 per cent.

Capital bonds

These attract interest at a rate that is fixed for 5 years and it is paid free of tax without the presentation of an Inland Revenue registration form. Bonds may be purchased in multiples of £100 with a maximum of £250,000. In 1993 the Series G bonds attracted a compound rate of interest of 7.75 per cent, but to achieve this the bond holder had to keep his bond intact for the 5-year period because the rate of interest rose during the 5 years as follows, 5.3 per cent, 5.9 per cent, 7.7 per cent, 9.0 per cent, 10.95 per cent, to give the overall yield of 7.75 per cent. The interest is added each year to the value of the bond, and at the end of the 5 years the bond is repaid in full with all the interest earned. No interest is paid if a bond is encashed before the first anniversary date and subsequently repayment is at the value of the bond on the last anniversary date plus interest to the date of repayment.

This bond is clearly meant for the investor who is looking for capital growth rather than for income.

Premium bonds

Premium bonds do not attract an annual rate of interest for the holder but instead a notional rate of interest on the total of all premium bonds is put into a pool from which weekly and monthly prizes are drawn. It is a gamble as to whether a particular investor will ever receive a prize, but at least his investment is protected and he can withdraw it at any time.

Winning bond numbers are selected at random by an electronic machine and each month there are some 160,000 prizes ranging from £50 to £250,000, whilst there are just three prizes at the weekly draw of £25,000, £50,000, and £100,000.

For an adult the minimum investment is £100 but for children the minimum is £10. Above these amounts bonds may be purchased in multiples of £10.

Children's bonus bonds

These bonds are especially suitable for parents, friends and relatives to give to children as gifts. They can be bought for any child under 16 and go on growing until he or she is 21. The interest is completely free of income tax whereas with other investments if a child's income from a gift from a parent exceeds £100 the parent is liable on it. Every 5 years up to the time when the child is 21 a substantial bonus is paid. The compound interest rate for the first 5 years is guaranteed at the outset (in 1993 Series E bonds were attracting 7.85 per cent) and at the end of that period a guaranteed rate of interest and bonus for the next 5 years is offered. For the first 5 years of the Series E bonds the rate of interest is 5 per cent with a bonus of 18.28 per cent on the fifth anniversary to make the average rate 7.85 per cent.

Government stock

The Department of Savings also provides a facility to buy up to £10,000 at a time of certain government stocks through what is called the National Savings Stock Register on very favourable terms. As we shall be dealing next with the Stock Exchange, through which sales and purchases of shares in companies and most dealings in government stocks are transacted, we shall defer our examination of the National Savings Stock Register until then.

Figure 3.3 shows the financial intermediaries in diagrammatic form.

Figure 3.3 Financial intermediaries

3.10 The Stock Exchange

Buying and selling stocks and shares

Many savers prefer to invest their money directly into stocks and shares rather than do so indirectly through financial intermediaries, such as insurance companies, unit trusts and investment trusts, all of which invest their policyholders' and investors' funds in government stocks and company shares. They are prepared to take the risk that the particular shares they choose turn out to be less successful than they expected, in terms of dividends that are paid and growth in the value of the shares. On the other hand, they are free to buy and sell shares as they please, and stand to get a great amount of satisfaction from managing their own portfolio of stocks and shares. However, buying and selling shares can be expensive for the small investor because stock dealers, although they charge a fee based on the value of the shares, impose a minimum charge. Stamp duty has also to be paid when shares are purchased.

A stock exchange is a market through which such purchases and sales can be arranged, and the London Stock Exchange is amongst the largest in the world. All British government stocks (usually referred to as British funds) are quoted on the Stock Exchange and also shares in public limited companies (plcs) which have applied for (and been granted) permission for their shares to be listed. Such a listing imposes an obligation upon the company to abide by the code of conduct laid down by the Stock Exchange Council concerning the way in which the company's affairs are conducted and dealings in its shares. If the Council is not satisfied, they have the right to suspend or discontinue the quotation of the company's shares.

When a company 'goes public' or wishes to raise capital its shares are offered for sale (see p. 29), and this will be done before the shares are quoted on the Stock Exchange. The exchange therefore deals in 'second-hand' shares but, nevertheless, it is a convenient channel through which savings can be invested in industry and commerce. Similarly, government funds are first issued by the Bank of England but in that a large proportion is usually taken up by the Bank of England itself in order to use the stock as a 'tap issue' (see below) the public sector can raise fresh funds through the Stock Exchange.

Stock dealers can perform either or both of two functions – as 'wholesalers' in particular types of shares, known as market makers, or as 'retailers' offering to buy or sell shares for or from their customers, known as stockbrokers. The large retail banks have subsidiary and associated companies which act both as stockbrokers and as market makers and there are some separate companies which perform one or both of these functions. A company which provides both services must keep its wholesale side quite separate from its retail side, and there are very strict rules about this.

As far as the bank customer is concerned, in placing his order over the bank counter or at one of the dealing screens located in some of the branches of the larger banks, he is dealing with the stockbroker with whom he places his order to buy or sell a quantity of stock or shares. For shares he will instruct the bank to buy or sell at the best available price on the market or, possibly, to hold the order and to buy or sell when the price has fallen to a particular level or has risen to a particular level for buying and selling respectively. When buying he may instruct the broker either to invest a specified sum in the shares or to buy a certain number of shares. He receives a written contract and for shares will have to pay for them, or receive a payment for them, on settlement day. The year is split up into account periods of 2 weeks (sometimes 3 weeks) ending on a Friday, and settlement day is 10 days later, on the Monday week after the end of the account. For purchases of government stocks the customer has to pay as soon as he receives the contract note.

Completion of the transfer of ownership of shares is done by the registrar (which may be a bank) of the company concerned, who issues a share certificate to the new owner indicating his or her name and address. This is not necessary for what are called bearer securities, which simply pass from hand to hand without registration of names.

The Bank of England, acting for the government, buys and sells government stocks through one of the stockbrokers. The Bank also handles new issues of government stocks and invites applications for them from the public direct (i.e. not through the Stock Exchange), and the banks and other financial institutions buy large amounts of them. Some of the latest issue of stock will always be kept by the Bank of England, however, to be made available for sale on the Stock Exchange as and when it is strategically appropriate to do so.

This particular stock is called the 'tap stock', a name derived from the fact that the Bank of England 'turns on the tap' and makes more of the stock available when it decides to do so. This device is useful in controlling the quantity of stocks available for sale on the Stock Exchange at any particular time, and through that influencing the prices of gilt-edged stocks and their yields. Inasmuch as the majority of government stocks are long-dated – i.e. they have many years to maturity – the government is able to influence the level of long-term interest rates through the Stock Exchange, as well as short-term interest rates through the discount market.

As mentioned in Section 3.9 above, some government stocks can be bought and sold through the National Savings Stock Register using forms that are available at post offices. The forms are sent by post to the Bonds and Stock Office at Blackpool and thus it takes a few days for the transaction to be completed. It is therefore not possible precisely to determine the price at which the stock will be bought or sold – the Stock Register simply undertakes to carry out the transaction at the market price for the stock at the time it receives the application. However, using the Stock Register has two advantages – the commission charges are much lower than they would be through a stock dealer (£4 per £1,000) and the interest on stocks bought in this way is paid gross whereas it is normally paid net of income tax.

The national newspapers list the dealing prices for British funds (government stocks) and company shares at the close of business each day. For each stock the broker will quote two prices – one is the price at which he is willing to sell; the other (lower) price is the buying price. The prices quoted in the press are the middle prices (and therefore, assuming that share prices have remained unchanged since the prices were quoted, the buyer must expect to pay a few pence more per share and the seller a few pence less per share).

The bank's stockbroker arm will not only buy and sell stocks and shares for the bank's customers but will also give advice about the suitability of particular stocks and shares for their needs.

The importance of the Stock Exchange

The Stock Exchange plays a very important role in the community in that it provides an efficient market for existing securities, through which securities can be converted into cash or into other assets. It enables savers – including the institutions such as pension funds, insurance companies, and unit trusts which collect other people's savings – to lend their money to industry and to the government. Borrowers and lenders are brought into touch with one another through the market.

Prices of stocks and shares on the Stock Exchange, together with their yields and information concerning the progress of the companies concerned, are published in the national press, and this information assists savers in deciding how to invest their funds. Movements in share prices are determined by supply and demand, and are a useful barometer of opinion as to the future prospects for industry and commerce and of the likely future trend for interest rates. A favourable opinion concerning the prospects for a particular company will cause the price of its shares to rise, and will make it easier (and cheaper) for the company concerned to raise new capital through a new share issue, should it wish to do so.

Both the government and industry have access through the Stock Exchange to the community's savings which they are able to tap respectively through the issue of stocks and shares.

3.1.1   The Money Market

Now that we have now looked in Chapters 2 and 3 at the various financial institutions that exist as intermediaries between those with funds to invest and those that wish to borrow, we are in a position to look at the money market as a whole. The institutions we looked at in Chapter 2, i.e. the banks, including the Bank of England, the retail banks, the merchant banks, foreign banks, and the discount houses together with the money brokers, comprise the main short-term money market. To this should be added the so-called 'parallel markets', i.e. the interbank market, the market in certificates of deposit, the Euro-currency market and the foreign exchange market which are, in the main, short-term markets. The institutions considered in this current chapter are more concerned with long-term investment, especially the building societies and the insurance companies, and the Stock Exchange also provides a channel for long-term investment in both industry and the government sector.

The Bank of England operates in the money market as a whole to carry out the government's monetary policy, but on occasions may concentrate its efforts on the short-term market through manipulating its own interest rate (the rate at which it is willing to lend to the discount houses) and through the supply of short-term assets such as Treasury bills and commercial bills, whilst at other times it will turn its attention more to the long-term market, influencing long-term interest rates by its issue and redemption of government stocks.

Review Questions

1   What is the main function of a building society? (3.2)
2   In what ways have the building societies been able to successfully compete with the banks in recent years? (3.2)
3   Do the building societies offer current accounts with cheque books? (3.2)
4   Can building societies lend for purposes other than house purchase? (3.2)
5   How would you distinguish between insurance and assurance? (3.3)
6   What is the function of Lloyds of London? (3.3)
7   What is the difference between the whole life and endowment policies? (3.3)
8   What is meant by term assurance? (3.3)
9   How does a pension fund operate? (3.3)
10 What is an annuity? (3.3)
11 What services are provided by the finance houses? (3.4)
12 Why might an individual choose to invest in a unit trust? (3.5)
13 What are the differences between a unit trust and an investment trust? (3.5, 3.6)
14 What is meant by a friendly society? (3.7)
15 What is a credit union? (3.8)
16 How would you distinguish between a National Savings Bank ordinary account and an investment account? (3.9)
17 What is a Savings Certificate? (3.9)
18 What is a National Savings Yearly Plan? (3.9)
19 Why might an individual choose to invest in an Income Bond? (3.9)
20 What are the differences between an Income Bond and a First Option Bond? (3.9)
21 What are the advantages to an investor of a Capital Bond? (3.9)
22 Does someone who 'gambles' on premium bonds stand to lose all of his money? (3.9)
23 What are the advantages of Children's Bonus Bonds? (3.9)
24 How can an individual invest in stocks and shares? (3.10)
25 What is meant by 'going public'? (3.10)
26 What is meant by 'settlement day'? (3.10)
27 How does the Bank of England issue government stocks? (3.10)
28 What are the advantages of buying stocks through the National Savings Stock Register? (3.10)
29 What is the main purpose of the Stock Exchange?
30 What is meant by the term 'money market'? Distinguish between the short-term and long-term money markets. (3.11)

Past Examination Questions

1   (a) Insurance companies provide protection for dependants and/or a
         means of saving for their policyholders. What life assurance policy
         would you recommend to the following types of customer? List
         three main features for each policy:
         (i)   Customers who want an effective savings plan with security
                for dependants. The policy should be capable of supporting a
                mortgage on a house.

                                                              (*4 marks*)
         (ii)   Customers who want to provide security for their dependants
                and have a lump sum payable only on their death.

                                                              (*4 marks*)
         (iii) Customers who want short-term cover that is relatively cheap.
                They are not worried about the savings aspect of assurance.

                                                              (*4 marks*)
     (b) Finance houses compete with banks in many areas of business. For
         each of the following customers state which service would be most
         appropriate. List three main features of the service:
         (i)   A self-employed gardener who needs a small excavator. He
                does not want to use capital to buy a machine and would like
                the maintenance and service to be taken into account.

                                                              (*4 marks*)
         (ii)   A young man buying his first second-hand car. He is aged 21,
                has a regular job and wants to pay for the car over 3 years. He
                does not have and does not want a bank account.

                                                              (*4 marks*)

2   The following are descriptions of types of financial institution. In each
     case identify the institution and then answer the questions which follow
     each description:
     (i)   'It borrows money from the public and lends mainly for house
            purchase.'
            Briefly explain this institution's areas of activity and list the main
            services under each activity.

                                                              (*10 marks*)
     (ii)   'It allows investors to pool their resources to be invested in a wide
            range of securities.'
            State the main purpose of this type of institution, explain what
            types of investment it provides and list two customer benefits.

                                                              (*6 marks*)
     (iii) 'It is a major competitor for personal savings and provides
            protection for dependants.'
            List six types of 'service' that this institution provides.

                                                              (*4 marks*)

Past Examination Questions   cont'd.

3   The following quotes identify competitors to the banks.

(a) 'The main type of competitor for "banking" business on the High Street.'
Name the type of organisation and list the services it provides under the headings of savings, loans, payment methods.

(8 marks)

(b) 'Provides a means of indirect stock market investment but is not a unit trust.'
What is this type of company called? Explain briefly how it works.

(5 marks)

(c) 'Although providing a banking service geared largely to small personal savers, it offers only limited services.'
Name the type of organisation and list the services it offers. Give two advantages and two disadvantages to the customer of using this organisation.

(7 marks)

---

4 The banker–customer relationship

┌─ Chapter objectives ───

When you have carefully studied this chapter you should be able to:
- Define a bank
- Define a bank customer
- Explain the relationships of debtor/creditor and principal/agent
- Explain the relationships of bailor/bailee and mortgagor/mortgagee
- Explain the special relationship that exists between banker and customer and the banker's rights and duties
- Give brief accounts of the main effects of the Consumer Credit Act 1974, the Financial Services Act 1986, and the Banking Acts of 1979 and 1987
- Explain the main recommendations of the Jack Committee concerning the banks' duty of confidentiality
- Explain the functions of the banking ombudsman

4.1 Introduction

In this chapter we will examine in some detail the very important part of the business of banking which is concerned with the relationship between the banker and his customer. To the person employed in banking a proper understanding of this vital aspect of his work is of course essential in that the banks have duties to their customers laid down, but at the same time have rights that protect them in their dealings both with and on behalf of the customers. The Jack Committee looked into both the law and practice of banking and in 1989 made recommendations, one result of which has been the preparation by the banks of a published code of conduct concerning their dealings with their customers. We shall need to look at this code as well as some of the other recommendations of the committee and the government's response to them.

We shall also need to look at some statute law and some case law to understand how they apply to banking. Statute law is that laid down by Parliament (i.e. in Acts of Parliament) whilst case law is based on the decisions of the courts over the years and holds good until some subsequent court amends it or until Parliament introduces a statute which overrides the case law.

4.2   What is a Bank?

Until the Banking Act 1979, statute law had not been very helpful in defining a bank. In fact the statutes seemed to dodge the issue in that several Acts of Parliament described a bank as a company or body corporate or partnership *carrying on the business of banking*! One court case in the 1960s was more helpful, however, in that the point at issue was whether a particular institution was carrying on the business of banking. That case was *United Dominions Trust Ltd* v. *Kirkwood* (1965). In the judgment relating to this case, three characteristics were held to be usually found in a banker's business. These were that banks are expected to:

1   Accept money from, and to collect cheques for, customers and to place the cheques to the customers' credit in a running account
2   Honour cheques or orders drawn on the bankers by their customers when presented for payment, and to debit their customers in the running account accordingly
3   Keep customers' running accounts in which credits and debits were entered

The 1979 Banking Act, as amended by the 1987 Act, has been quite specific about what is required of an institution before it can call itself a bank. The 1979 Act required such institution to:

1   Have enjoyed a high reputation and standing in the financial community for a reasonable period of time
2   Provide a wide range of banking services or a highly specialised banking service
3   Have net assets of at least £5 million

As to what is regarded as a 'wide range of banking services' the Act was also quite specific:

1   Current or deposit account facilities or the acceptance of funds in the wholesale money markets
2   Finance in the form of overdraft or loan facilities or the lending of funds in the wholesale money markets
3   Foreign exchange services for domestic and foreign customers
4   Finance through the medium of bills of exchange and promissory notes, together with finance for foreign trade and documentation in connection with foreign trade
5   Financial advice or investment management services and facilities for arranging the purchase and sale of securities

The 1979 Act gave the Bank of England discretion as far as to how many of these services a particular institution offers. The 1987 Act stipulates that a bank must be a deposit-taking institution under the Act and reaffirms that it must have net assets of at least £5 million. An institution with assets of less than £5 million (but at least £1 million) may become an authorised deposit-taking institution, but is not permitted to call itself a bank. All authorised deposit-taking institutions must have fit and proper people as directors, must be effectively directed by at least two individuals, and must conduct their business in a prudent manner.

4.3   What is a Customer?

Whereas, as we have seen, there is now a statutory definition of a bank, there is no statutory definition of a bank customer and therefore it is necessary to rely on case law in order to establish whether or not a person is a customer. In *Great Western Railway* v. *London and County Banking Co.* (1901), it was stated that a customer must have a current or deposit account or some similar relationship. However not all 'customers' of banks deposit money and may, for instance, deposit valuables other than money, yet the banks regard such people as customers. In *Woods* v. *Martins Bank Ltd and Another* (1959) it was considered that Woods became a customer when he made an investment in a company on the advice of the manager, even though his account was not opened for some weeks thereafter.

The length of time during which there have been dealings with a person does not appear to affect the situation, for in *Ladbroke and Co.* v. *Todd* (1914) and *Commissioners of Taxation* v. *English, Scottish and Australian Bank Ltd* (1920), it was established that a continuous dealing relationship was not essential to a definition of a customer and that the relationship began immediately an account was opened and funds paid into it.

The time of commencement of the banker–customer relationship is important because the contractual duties of a banker do not begin until then and, furthermore, to gain protection of s.4 of the Cheques Act 1957 when collecting a cheque, the bank must receive payment **for a customer**.

4.4   Basic Contractual Relationship

The banker–customer relationship has been largely left to implied contract, the terms of which have been developed by judicial decisions over the years (i.e. by case law). Furthermore, much of the case law is quite old and has changed very little over time. The term 'implied contract' means that there is no written agreement between the bank and its customer, and their relationship is simply based on what has happened between banks and their customers in the past and the decisions that the courts have made when the banks have been sued for failure to fulfil their implied obligations.

Debtor and creditor

The contract between a customer and the bank is normally that of debtor and creditor, the bank being the debtor because it owes money to the depositor and the customer is the creditor because he is owed money (see Figure 4.1). However, this is the situation only when the account is in credit and if it is overdrawn the bank is the creditor and the customer is the debtor.

Account In Credit	Bank is **DEBTOR**
	Customer is **CREDITOR**
Account Overdrawn	Bank is **CREDITOR**
	Customer is **DEBTOR**

Figure 4.1   The contractual relationship

It is normal practice in the UK for the debtor to have to seek out the creditor and repay him, but this does not apply to the banks when as debtors they hold depositors' funds. Instead it is up to the depositor to demand repayment when he requires it. When an account is overdrawn the normal relationship of debtor (the customer) and creditor (the bank) applies, and it is up to the customer, as debtor, to seek out his creditor to repay him.

Principal and agent

When the bank acts on behalf of its customer – when, for instance, it collects a cheque on his behalf – it does so as the customer's agent, and the customer is known as the principal. A similar situation arises when the bank remits funds abroad or buys stocks and shares for the customer. There are times when these roles are reversed – as, for instance, when the bank holds a letter of pledge over goods which the customer is importing, and the bank allows the customer access to those goods against a trust receipt. In the trust receipt the customer undertakes to act on behalf of the bank when handling the goods and to pay the proceeds from selling the goods over to the bank. When the relationship of principal and agent exists between the bank and its customer the law of agency applies as well as the normal law of contract.

Bailor and bailee

When banks take charge of deed boxes, parcels of deeds, stocks and shares and other securities on behalf of their customers they are **bailees**. If the banker is paid for this service he is a **bailee for reward**, but otherwise he is a **gratuitous bailee**, and this distinction between the two types could make some difference should there be an accusation of negligence against a bank by a customer as **bailor** of property lodged with the bank for safe custody – a gratuitous bailee must take reasonable care of property entrusted, but a paid bailee must take the maximum possible care, including modern security devices, when looking after property. However, the distinction between the two types of bailees has become less important because the banks do take very good care of property left with them, and these days they are nearly always bailees for reward because they charge their customers for safe custodies. Whether paid bailees or not, it is incumbent upon the banker as bailee to prove that the loss of any property bailed was not the fault of the bank or its agents. Another important factor these days is that the banks insist that when a customer deposits something for safe custody he makes sure that the property is covered by his own domestic insurance policy whilst the goods are in the bank's care.

If an item left in safe custody is delivered to the wrong person, the banker could be sued for conversion, which is an unauthorised act that deprives another person of his property. We shall come across this term again later in this book in connection with the collection of cheques.

When property is deposited with a bank for safe custody the bailor (the customer) retains ownership of it, and the bank cannot claim a lien on it (a right to retain possession of another's property until the owner pays a debt), except to the extent of any unpaid fees in respect of the bailment itself. This means that if the customer has a loan or overdraft which is unsecured or inadequately secured, the bank cannot claim possession of property on safe custody as security for the debt.

Banks prefer boxes to be locked and packages to be sealed before they are lodged for safekeeping and the bank's receipt usually states that the contents are unknown. These precautions may lessen the bank's liability for loss or damage.

Mortgagor and mortgagee

When a customer mortgages his house to his bank or to a building society he is the **mortgagor** and the bank or building society is the **mortgagee**. A mortgage can take the form of a full legal charge over the property or simply an equitable charge. The former involves registering a signed legal document with the Land Registry (unless it is unregistered land), whereas the latter simply involves depositing the land certificate or deeds with the bank together with the bank's form of equitable mortgage which is signed by the mortgagor.

The property that is mortgaged need not be land and, for example, a charge taken over stocks and shares is in fact a mortgage.

The special relationship

Beyond the contractual relationships we have considered the banks are regarded as having a special relationship with their customers which arises from the degree of trust which customers have in their banks. In view of this trust the banks must be extremely careful in their dealings with their customers and must not put themselves in a position where it could be claimed that they have exerted undue influence over a customer. Two fairly recent court cases highlight this special relationship.

In *Lloyds Bank* v. *Bundy* (1975) Bundy, an elderly gentleman with a lack of business acumen, guaranteed his son's overdraft under advice from his bank which was the same bank as his son's. There was a series of guarantees involved and they were supported by mortgages over his farm property. At one stage he was told that unless he signed a further guarantee, which he did, the bank would call in his son's overdraft. In the event a receiving order was made against the son and the bank attempted to call in the guarantee and to take over the farmhouse. The court upheld Bundy's attempt to set aside the guarantee and the charge over the security on the grounds that the bank had exercised undue influence. It declared that the bank had to disprove that there had been undue influence, and had not succeeded in doing so.

In *National Westminster Bank* v. *Morgan* (1985), which was taken as far as the House of Lords, Mrs Morgan claimed undue influence on the part of the bank when she was persuaded to sign a further mortgage over her house. The final decision in this case was in the bank's favour because the bank's loan had saved the Morgans from having the house repossessed by a building society. The court referred to the Bundy case and said that to succeed in a claim of undue influence the plaintiff must establish that a dominant position of trust had been misused and that the plaintiff, the weaker party, had suffered as a consequence. In the previous case this was definitely so but in this case the plaintiff's position had actually improved as a result of signing the further mortgage.

4.5   Bankers' Rights and Duties

The banks' responsibilities towards their customers have largely been dictated by case law, as have their rights, and it is therefore necessary to look at individual cases when considering these rights and duties (see Figure 4.2).

In *Joachimson* v. *Swiss Bank Corporation* (1921) the court reviewed the duties of a banker and said that:

1   The banker must receive money from and collect cheques and other bills of exchange from the customer and repay the money against the customer's written order. The order must be addressed to the branch where the account is kept and repayment made at that branch during normal working hours (banking practice has changed since then, of course, in that, for instance,

Banker **MUST**	Banker **MUST NOT**
Receive Deposits	Pay a Cheque Where:
Collect Cheques and Bills of Exchange	Signature is Forged
Repay Customer upon it's Written or Electronic Instruction	Signature is Missing
Give Reasonable Notice When Closing Account	There is a Material Alteration that is not Signed or Initialled by Customer
Exercise Care in Carrying out Customer's Instructions	Payment has been Countermanded
Keep Accurate Records	Customer has Died
Provide Statements of Account	Notice of Bankruptcy has been Received
Notify Customer of Forgery	Receiving Order has been Made
Keep Customer's Affairs Confidential	Court Injuction has been Received
Follow the Usual Banking Practice	

Banker MAY

Return Cheque Unpaid If There Are Insufficient Funds

Pay a Cheque For Amount in Words if Words and Figures Differ but Alternatively, Could Return it Unpaid

Use Funds Deposited as it Thinks Fit

Figure 4.2   Bankers' rights and duties

such orders may be given by pressing the keys at a service till after hours, and we shall need to consider this matter later).

2   The banker must give reasonable notice before closing an account in order that the customer may make other arrangements and also so that any cheques that may have been drawn may reach the bank.

With regard to the first of these duties, the bank must exercise reasonable competence and care in carrying out the customer's instructions. So too must the customer, as was clearly demonstrated in the case of *London Joint Stock Bank* v. *McMillan and Arthur* (1918), where an employee of a customer wrote out a cheque for £2 but did not insert the words and left sufficient space either side of the figure 2 for amount of the cheque to be altered after signature by the customer to £120. It was held that the bank's customer (the employer) did not exercise reasonable care in making the written order, and therefore lost his case against the bank. Since then the banks have carefully advised their customers on cheque books and by other means to be careful in writing their cheques. For instance, in a pamphlet to customers concerning the introduction of 'Account Payee' cheques (see p. 95) NatWest advises its customers to 'Write your cheques clearly with the Payee's name and the amount in words and figures starting as far as possible to the left of the space provided so that other words and figures cannot be inserted. Fill in any unused spaces with a thick line'.

Also concerning the first of these duties above, the case of *Whitehead* v. *National Westminster Bank* (1982) can be cited. This case involved another form of customer's order to pay i.e. a standing order (see p. 111). Whitehead had failed to ensure that sufficient funds were in his account to meet standing order payments to his building society and in consequence the bank did not make a number of the monthly payments although sufficient funds were paid in after the due dates. It was held that it was not the duty of the bank to hold standing order payments until sufficient funds were received. The duty was to make the payments on the due dates and not to wait until funds were paid in.

With regard to the second of the responsibilities highlighted in the *Joachimson* case, the question of what is reasonable notice when closing an account came up in the case *Prosperity Ltd* v. *Lloyds Bank* (1923). The bank had given its customer 1 month in which to close the account but the court ruled that the bank was in breach of contract when closing the account at the expiry of that period because the period of notice was insufficient. However, the customer's account was a very active and complicated one and it is likely that 1 month's notice would be considered adequate for a more straightforward account.

It has always been assumed that the banker has the implied right to charge interest on advances, and reasonable commission for other services performed for a customer. The bank is also entitled to be reimbursed for any expenses incurred in acting on a customer's behalf. The banker has the right to repayment on demand of any overdrawn balance and has the right to exercise a lien (see p. 58) over any of the customer's property lodged with the bank other than that simply deposited for safe custody. The lien covers negotiable instruments such as cheques and bills of exchange, and any other document which provides for money to be paid to the customer, such as an insurance policy. Regulations concerning liquidity and prudential use of funds are laid down by the Bank of England under its powers given in the Banking Acts 1979 and 1987. Provided a bank satisfies these requirements it is free to use its customers' money as it thinks fit. This was established in *Foley* v. *Hill* (1848), in which it was held that a bank can use customers' money as its own provided it is repaid on customer demand.

A bank must keep accurate records and provide its customer with statements of account. It must also advise the customer immediately if a forgery on a cheque is drawn to its attention and must not pay such a cheque (see Chapter 6). In the case of *Brown* v. *Westminster Bank* (1964), the bank had checked with its customer on a number of occasions as to the genuineness of the signature on a large number of cheques drawn on his account and he had said that they were genuine. In fact they had been signed by his wife. He later sued the bank for negligence in paying the forged cheques but the court ruled that having once claimed that the signatures were genuine he could not now claim that they were forgeries, and he lost the case.

It has always been understood that a bank has a responsibility to keep his customer's affairs confidential and, as we shall see in Section 4.6 this has been dealt with both in a leading case and by the Jack Committee.

Finally, it has always been made clear in the courts that a banker must act in the normal course of business. This means that the customer must be able to expect his bank to follow the normal recognised practice within the banking industry. There is a serious complication here in that banking practice continually changes, witness for example the changes that have occurred in recent years in bank opening hours and in which there is a great deal of inconsistency: some bank branches are still closed at 3.30 p.m. whilst others go on to a later hour, and not all branches are open on Saturday mornings.

The Jack Committee's Report 'Banking Services; Law and Practice' (1989) reviewed the duties of care on bankers, and said that the banker's duty to obey his customer's mandate could be said to be supplemented by a more general duty of care implied by common law. The report looked at case law right up to the time it was written and concluded with the judgment in the appeal in the case *Lipkin Gorman* v. *Karpnale and Lloyds Bank* (1988), which explicitly questioned earlier judgments and criticised some of them as stating the common law duty of care on bankers too highly. The following is an extract from that judgment.

> The relationship between the parties is contractual. The principal obligation is upon the bank to honour its customer's cheques in accordance with its mandate or instructions. There is nothing in such a contract, express or implied, which could require a banker to consider the commercial wisdom or otherwise of the particular transaction. Nor is there normally any express term in the contract requiring the banker to exercise any degree of care in deciding whether to honour a customer's cheque which his instructions require him to pay. In my opinion any implied term requiring the banker to exercise care must be limited. To a substantial extent the banker's obligation under such a contract is largely

automatic or mechanical. Presented with a cheque drawn in accordance with the terms of that contract, the banker must honour it save in what I would expect to be exceptional circumstances.

We shall be looking at the cheques system in some detail in Chapter 6 and this will include a discussion of the circumstances in which a banker is justified in returning a cheque unpaid.

To sum up the banker's rights and duties, a banker must:

1 Receive money from, and collect cheques and other bills of exchange for, a customer and use these funds as he thinks fit provided that he satisfies the liquidity requirements of the Bank of England
2 Repay money against the customer's written order, (and, these days, against his use of a plastic service card)
3 Give reasonable notice before closing an account
4 Exercise reasonable competence and care in carrying out the customer's instructions; but this also means that the banker has the right to expect the customer to exercise reasonable care in drawing his cheques
5 Keep accurate records and provide his customer with statements of account
6 Not pay any cheque on which the customer's signature is forged and notify the customer immediately if such a forgery is drawn to his attention
7 Keep his customer's affairs confidential
8 Follow the usual banking practice

In addition the banker has the right to:

1 Charge interest on advances and reasonable commission for other services, and to be reimbursed for any expenses incurred in acting on the customer's behalf
2 To have repayment on demand of any overdrawn balance
3 To have a lien over any of the customer's property lodged with the bank other than on safe custody, and this includes cheques and other bills of exchange deposited for collection

Note that in Figure 4.2 the banker's duties when paying a cheque have been included – we shall be dealing with these in Chapter 6.

4.6 The Bond of Secrecy

Bank customers have always expected their affairs to be kept secret – quite apart from the legal responsibility of a bank to do so – and generally speaking this bond is rarely broken. However, there are occasions when a bank must divulge information about its customer's account even without express consent. In the case of *Tournier* v. *National Provincial Bank Ltd* (1924), it was decided that the duty of secrecy is not absolute, and that there are four instances when disclosure may be justified.

The Tournier exceptions (see Figure 4.3)

Under compulsion of law   A bank may be directed by a court to produce copies of a customer's account. Subsequent legislation has also compelled banks to divulge information, for instance, to inspectors authorised to investigate the affairs of companies, and to the Inland Revenue about credit interest on accounts in excess of a minimum amount in any one financial year.

Duty to the public   Where it is vital to the community – for instance, where a customer is known to be trading with an enemy country.

In the interests of the bank   Where, for instance, the bank is demanding payment from a guarantor of a customer's overdrawn account.

Where the customer's interest demands disclosure   Where, for instance, a bank replies to a status enquiry concerning its customer: here it is assumed that the bank has implied authority, if not written authority, from its customer. Similarly, where the bank is dealing with the manager of a business, there may be an implied consent on the part of the owners of the business to divulge information concerning the account.

The Jack Committee's views on confidentiality

The Jack Committee stated in its report that there was wide concern that the four exceptions were not closely enough defined for today's conditions, and that therefore they were potentially open to abuse. As far as the first two exceptions are concerned, there has been a torrent of new legislation requiring or permitting bankers to disclose confidential information in the public interest, caused by concern, for instance, about insider dealing, company fraud, insolvency, drug trafficking, breaches of the Consumer Credit Act, tax evasion, inquiries into the affairs of charities, extradition, and mental incapacity.

With reference to the second two exceptions, concern was expressed at the growing perception by some banks that they are entitled to release confidential information about customers to other companies within their own group, which in some cases are not banking companies. Concern was also expressed at the growth of credit reference companies and the possible disclosure of confidential information to them by banks. The banks had in fact, under pressure from the government, agreed to make 'black' information available to credit reference agencies. This is information about customers who are in default, as distinct from 'white' information about customers who are not. At the time the banks issued a

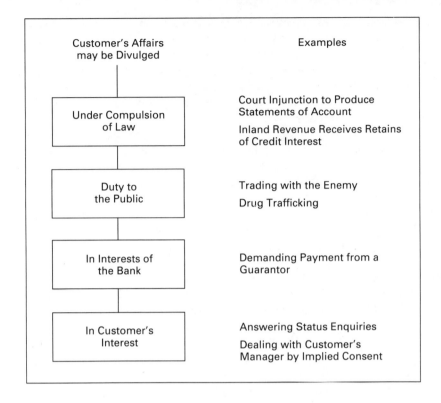

Figure 4.3   The *Tournier* exceptions

notice to their customers saying that they would supply information about debts normally up to £5,000, which are in default, where no security has been given and on which no satisfactory response has been received from the customer within 28 days of formal demand for repayment. There were also suggestions from the government that the banks should consider releasing white information as well, in order to ensure that the consumer credit industry operated in the interests of the lenders, of the borrowers, and of the industry as a whole. The Jack Committee expressed concern that white information should be made available in this way without customers' express consent and also recommended that the government should introduce fresh legislation that should take the following revisions of the *Tournier* exceptions into account:

1   The duty of confidentiality itself should be defined in the terms laid down by the Appeal Judges in the *Tournier* case, taking the majority view where there are points of judicial difference. The statute should make clear that the duty applies to any provider of banking services, and that it covers all information which the bank has acquired about the customer in the course of providing such services to him.

2   Under the first *Tournier* exception, where disclosure is under compulsion by law, all existing statutory exemptions should be consolidated in the new legislation. All new statutory exemptions from the duty of confidentiality should be made by reference to this new provision and if they did not accord with it they would not override the central duty of confidentiality.

3   The second *Tournier* exception, where there is a duty to the public to disclose, should be deleted.

4   The third *Tournier* exception, where the interests of the bank require disclosure, should be limited to (i) disclosure to a court in the event of legal action to which the bank is a party, (ii) disclosure as between banking companies within the same group, and (iii) disclosure in connection with the sale of the bank itself.

5   The fourth *Tournier* exception should be altered to read 'Where disclosure is made by the express consent of the customer'. This consent must be in writing and must state the purpose for which it has been given. The only relaxation of that requirement, to be spelled out in the legislation, is in the limited case of bankers' opinions where consent in tacit form should be obtained. The customer must be made clearly aware of the purpose for which such consent is required and be advised that such consent will be assumed unless he has within a reasonable time informed that bank that he does not wish to give it.

6   A new exception to the *Tournier* list of exceptions should be added. This reads 'Where there has been a breakdown of the banker–customer relationship arising through customer default'. Default should be defined as the case where no security has been given, and no satisfactory response has been received from the customer within 28 days of formal demand for repayment. Disclosure under such circumstances should be limited to the release of information to approved credit reference agencies.

7   The legislation should provide that for a breach of confidentiality under any of these rules damages should include compensation for distress, embarrassment or inconvenience, regardless of whether financial loss could be proved.

In addition to these recommendations concerning legislation, the Committee recommended that a standard of best practice drawn up by the banks should explain to the customers the rules on the banker's duty of confidentiality, once codified in statute law. It should remind customers of their right of access, under the Data Protection Act 1984, to computer records about themselves held by the banks. It should state that express consent, in whatever form, should not be sought in such a way as to put the customer under pressure to give it. In the case of express consent to be obtained in tacit form for the giving of bankers' opinions, a letter should be sent personally to its customer seeking his consent for this specific purpose.

Finally, the Committee recommended that the government should not extend the statutory exceptions to the duty of confidentiality without taking full account of the consequences for the banker–customer relationship.

The government's response to the Jack Committee's recommendations concerning confidentiality was to say that it saw no need to codify the present rules on confidentiality in statute, but thought it desirable that the code of banking practice which it was inviting the banks to draw up (see p. 69) should inform banks' customers of the existence of the rules (the *Tournier* rules). The code should also lay down good practice on the use of information for marketing purposes and the procedures for passing information to credit reference agencies. In taking this action on the report, the government said that it was persuaded by the evidence given during the Committee's consultations by those who argued that the so-called *Tournier* rules were clear, had worked well, and are widely understood by bankers and that any attempt to codify them in legislation would be at best unnecessary and at worst likely to introduce new difficulties and confusion. Furthermore, the government could not agree that there had been a massive erosion of the banker's duty of confidentiality through the various statutory exceptions to the general duty of confidentiality such as those in the Drug Trafficking Act 1986. These exceptions, it claimed, affect only the very small number of customers who use the banking system for dishonest purposes and have no impact on the vast majority of honest customers. Also, before enacting such exceptions, the government always considers with great care the implications, including the impact on banking confidentiality. The government enacts such exceptions only when necessary and where the benefits outweigh any possible disadvantages.

4.7   The Consumer Credit Act 1974

The Consumer Credit Act, as amended in 1985, established a code of conduct for the provision of consumer credit to individuals and businesses other than limited companies and other corporate bodies. It is concerned with advances, debt adjustment, debt counselling and debt collection but does not apply to transactions over £15,000. The two main provisions of the Act that affect the banks are concerned with canvassing and with the need for written agreements.

Canvassing

The Act makes it an offence to canvass for an advance or associated activity away from the canvasser's trade premises, and this includes bank branches. However, if the bank customer initiates a visit to his premises to discuss an advance the canvassing is deemed to be at the customer's request and is permitted under the Act. The provisions of the Act do not as a rule apply to telephone conversations, letters and circulars, except that it is an offence to send a document to a minor which invites the use of credit facilities. The Act makes it an offence to send a credit card to someone without a formal request to do so.

Written agreements

For any advance there must be a written agreement signed at the lender's premises. This agreement must include a statement of interest and all other charges as well as the true interest rate. The total charge has to be expressed as **an annual percentage rate** (APR), and this must include not only the pure interest charge but also any ancillary charges. A copy of the agreement must be given to the borrower and he has the right to cancel the agreement within a period of 5 days from the date of receiving it.

Connected lender liability

A further provision of the Act which affects the banks is that under the Act a credit card company shares responsibility with the supplier of goods or services paid for by the use of a credit card. This means that the credit card company is equally liable for any defect in the goods or services, but this applies only if the transaction is for £100 or more.

4.8   Financial Services Act 1986

This Act authorises the Department of Trade and Industry to regulate businesses concerned with investment. All such businesses have to satisfy safeguards laid down to protect investors' funds. The types of businesses involved are dealers in securities, investment advisers and managers, and those concerned with selling other financial services such as insurance and unit trusts.

One of the most important consequences of this Act affecting the banks was the establishment of the Securities and Investments Board (SIB) to regulate institutions in the financial markets. Under SIB the banks (and building societies) must choose between giving independent financial advice about financial services and selling only their own financial services. Of the big banks only NatWest has opted to provide independent advice and most of the other banks and building societies sell only their own services. The main purpose of this distinction between the two types of institution is that if it sells only its own financial services an institution is not likely to give unbiased advice about the financial products of other institutions.

There are a number of self-regulatory bodies set up at the instigation of the SIB and recognised by that Board:

- FIMBRA (Financial Intermediaries, Managers and Brokers' Regulatory Association)
- LAUTRO (Life Assurance and Unit Trust Regulatory Organisation)

- TSA   (The Securities Association) – all members of the Stock Exchange are members of this association.
- IMRO   (Investment Management Regulatory Organisation)

4.9   Banking Code of Practice

In March 1992 the banks, building societies and the card issuers published a voluntary code of practice as recommended by the Jack Committee. The code was prepared by the British Bankers' Association, the Building Societies Association and the Association for Payment Clearing Services (APACS). It lays down the minimum standard of banking practice with particular emphasis on the customer's rights. Some of the individual banks have published their own terms and conditions complying with the principles contained in the code.

The governing principles of the code are:

1 To set out the standards of good banking practice which the banks (and building societies and card issuers) are to follow in their dealings with their customers
2 That the banks will act fairly and reasonably in all their dealings with their customers
3 That the banks will help their customers to understand how their accounts operate and will seek to give them a good understanding of banking services
4 To maintain confidence in the security and the integrity of banking and card payment systems

The code requires banks to provide certain information to customers, usually at the time the account is opened, and to provide additional information and guidance about specific services on request. It also specifies the practice for the following:

- The procedure for identifying **new customers**
- The terms and conditions of a **banking service**
- **Charges and interest**
- Handling customers' **complaints**
- **Confidentiality** of customer information
- Bankers' **references**
- **Marketing of services**
- **Marketing and provision of credit**
- Details to customers as to how accounts **operate**
- **Foreign exchange** services
- **Guarantees** and other types of **third party security**
- Liability for loss by cardholders and other matters concerned with the issue of **plastic cards**

4.10   The Banking Ombudsman

As with the insurance and building society industries, the banking industry has an ombudsman to whom complaints can be referred by bank customers if they feel that their complaint has not been dealt with in a satisfactory manner by the bank concerned. Unlike the other two ombudsman schemes, membership is on a voluntary basis. This fact was criticised by the Jack Committee, which recommended that a statutory compulsory scheme should replace the voluntary scheme. The government did not put this proposal into effect, however, but said that it welcomed the attempt that was being made to encourage more banks to enter the scheme.

The ombudsman will deal with a complaint only if it has already been taken up with the bank concerned and the customer has not been satisfied. He can deal only with complaints from personal customers, but this does include sole traders, partnerships, and clubs and societies.

Complaints must be concerned about the bank's procedures and not about any business decision, and the majority of referrals to the ombudsman have been about bank charges, failure of an ATM to work properly, and poor administration.

Review Questions

1   Which court case was particularly helpful in providing a definition of a bank? What definition did it give? (4.2)
2   How did the Banking Act 1979, as amended by the 1987 Act, define a bank? (4.2)
3   Can anyone be a director of a bank, or are there special conditions laid down? (4.2)
4   Must a 'customer' of a bank have an account with that bank? (4.3)
5   Is a continuous dealing relationship essential to a definition of a customer? (4.3
6   Why is the definition of a customer so important in connection with the protection available to a banker? (4.3)
7   What is meant by an implied contract? (4.4)
8   What is meant by case law? (4.4)
9   What is meant by statute law? (4.4))
10   What is the debtor/creditor relationship between a bank and its customer? (4.4)
11   Does a bank, as debtor, have to seek out its creditor to repay him? What is the position if the customer is overdrawn? (4.4)
12   What is meant by the relationship of principal and agent? How does this apply in banking? (4.4)
13   When a bank looks after a deed box on behalf of a customer is it bailor or bailee? (4.4)

Review Questions cont'd.

14 How would you distinguish between a gratuitous bailee and a bailee for reward? (4.4)

15 What is meant by the legal term 'conversion'? (4.4)

16 How would you distinguish between the terms mortgagor and mortgagee? (4.4)

17 What is the special relationship that exists between a bank and its customer? (4.4)

18 What duties of a bank were specified in the Joachimson case? (4.5)

19 Why must a customer be careful when drawing a cheque? Refer to the case in which the court gave a ruling about this. (4.5)

20 Have the banks taken any action about the responsibility of customers to be careful in writing cheques? (4.5)

21 If a customer does not ensure that there are sufficient funds on his account on the day that a standing order payment is due to be made, must the bank delay payment until funds are paid in, or can it simply refuse to make the payment? State the case that applies here. (4.5)

22 What is meant by 'reasonable notice' when closing a customer's account? (4.5)

23 . Is a bank entitled to make charges on an account? If so, what may they be for? (4.5)

24 What is meant by a lien over a customer's property? (4.5)

25 Is a bank obliged to supply its customer with a statement of account? (4.5)

26 Must a bank take action if it suspects that a customer's signature on a cheque has been forged? (4.5)

27 Is it important that a bank should act within the normal course of business? (4.5)

28 What did the Jack Committee have to say about the banker's duty of care? (4.5)

29 It has always been understood that a bank must keep its customers' affairs confidential. Are there any exceptions to this rule? (4.6)

30 What did the Jack Committee have to say about the duty of confidentiality? (4.6)

31 How did the government react to the Jack Committee's recommendations on confidentiality? (4.6)

32 How did the provisions of the Consumer Credit Act affect the banks? (4.7)

33 What were the consequences of the Financial Services Act 1986 for the banks? (4.8)

34 What do the following initials stand for:
FIMBRA, LAUTRO, TSA, IMRO? (4.8)

35 What is the function of the banking ombudsman? (4.10)

Past Examination Questions

1   Supporting your answer with examples from statute and case law define:
     (a) a bank   (*12 marks*)
     (b) a customer.   (*8 marks*)

2   Your branch receives the following letter. Reply to the customer by letter, explaining what you are required to do.

Dear Sir,

I have recently opened an account and have been told that you can charge for services and receive interest on loans. You can apparently use my money in any way you like provided you honour my cheques.

I also understand that you are required to perform certain moral and legal duties as part of our relationship. Would you please explain what these are.

Yours faithfully

C. Plane (Mrs)   (*20 marks*)

3   State (a) the rights, and   (*6 marks*)
           (b) the duties of a banker   (*14 marks*)
     To gain full marks, candidates must do more than write down a list.

4   A school has asked you to talk to the senior pupils to allay their fears that if they opened an account with your (or any) bank they would have little protection. One of the pupils has said, 'Banks can do as they please and seem to feel that they owe nothing to their customers'.

     How would you explain to them that if banks and customers are to do business then relationships need to be established? *Write notes* on these relationships, and state what duties banks owe to their customers.
                                                                  (*20 marks*)

5 | Bank customers

┌─ **Chapter objectives** ───
When you have carefully studied this chapter you should be able to:
- Define the different types of personal accounts
- Examine the different types of business account and the advantages and disadvantages to the businessman of operating as a sole trader, in a partnership, and within a company
- Explain the procedures for opening each type of account
└──

5.1 Introduction

In this chapter we will examine in detail the idiosyncrasies of each type of bank customer and the procedures for opening each type of account. These procedures range from a simple mandate form for the private individual at one extreme to the rather complicated formalities required when a company is established and wishes to open an account. In each case, the bank must seek to guard itself against any action on the part of the customer(s) which might jeopardise its protection (under the Cheques Act 1957, for instance), in any claim against it for conversion, negligence or breach of contract. It must also ensure that it establishes joint and several liability if more than one party is involved with an account, and that in the event of the death, bankruptcy or liquidation, or mental incapacity of any customer, it has proper redress for any debit balance.

5.2 Personal Accounts

Opening accounts

The application form   There is a wide range of accounts available to the would-be customer of a bank, and he makes a choice on the basis of his particular needs. If he (or she) wishes simply to deposit money and earn interest on it, then a deposit or investment account would be appropriate. If the ability to draw cheques and maybe to use an ATM is wanted, then a current account would be necessary. If he wishes to use a debit card or a credit card, then it may be necessary to open a special type of current account for the purpose. We shall look at the use of plastic cards in some detail in Chapter 10.

Whichever type of account is opened, an application form will have to be completed by the customer. These vary according to the type of account and as between banks, but the basic information required will include the person's full name, address and occupation whichever form is used, and the customer will be required to give one or more specimen signatures for the bank's records in order that his signature can be verified when necessary. If you are employed in a bank, do look at the various types of application form used by your bank.

Identity and character   When a would-be account holder is known to the bank or is introduced by an existing customer, the bank may well decide that it need take no further action to identify him or to require someone to vouch for his suitability to be a customer. If a complete stranger walks into the bank and asks to open an account then it is a different matter. First of all it is necessary to identify him. He may well be able to satisfy the bank on this score by producing some evidence of identity such as his driving licence or, preferably, some document such as his passport on which there is a photograph of him. He is unlikely to carry his passport about with him, however, and may object to being asked to produce it. The reason why the bank must be cautious is that he may be masquerading as some other person and subsequently pay in cheques payable to that person. If the bank collects payment of such cheques for him it may be successfully sued by the true owner for conversion (see p. 58 for a definition of this), and especially so if it can be shown that the bank was negligent when opening the account.

The bank is often helped in identifying the customer by the facts that he gives about his occupation and a request that he be allowed to have his salary paid directly into his account. He may also give details of a number of standing orders and direct debits that he wishes to establish from which it may be gleaned that he is in fact the householder at the address given, e.g. he may be arranging for his monthly mortgage payments to be made. Such information also helps to establish his financial status, which will hopefully be confirmed once the size of his first salary payment is known. This information is valuable, not only in deciding the person's suitability as a bank customer, but also when possibly at a later stage he asks to borrow money from the bank.

Usually potential customers are willing to give helpful information when opening an account, but if the bank is not satisfied as to the identity and financial status of the stranger it will need to look elsewhere for help. It could refer to one of the credit reference agencies for information they may have as to his credit rating, but this is not always reliable and must be used with care. Alternatively, the bank may require from him the names and addresses of one or two persons who would be willing to act as referees on his behalf. If one of these is the customer's employer all well and good because this will not only identify him but may also establish the nature of his employment.

Because of the very heavy volume of work the bigger banks have tended to take the risk of not taking up references in recent years and the Jack Committee had something to say about this. Before looking at the Committee's comments, however, it would be sensible briefly to examine the case law on the subject because over a long period of years the banks have frequently been sued for conversion and the courts have tended to rule heavily against them where it has been shown that the banks have been careless when opening accounts for strangers.

The case law   In *Ladbroke and Co.* v. *Todd* (1914) the bank was successfully sued for conversion because it did not obtain references in respect of a new customer unknown to the bank.

In the cases *Guardians of St John's Hampstead* v. *Barclays Bank* (1923) and *Lumsden and Co.* v. *London Trustee Savings Bank* (1971) where references were taken up, the banks were nevertheless successfully sued because they did not check on the authenticity of the references. In both cases the customer gave a false name and the reference was forged. In the first case the thief pretended that his name was Donald Stewart and at a later date paid in stolen cheques payable to Donald Stewart & Co. claiming that he traded in that name. The bank did not check that either an individual of that name or a firm of that name were at the address given by him. In an endeavour to avoid forged references the banks frequently ask for details of the referee's bank and request a report from that bank as to his suitability to act as a referee.

We shall examine the case law further in Chapter 6 in relation to the duties of the banker who is collecting a cheque for a customer.

The comments of the Jack Committee   The Committee refers to the decline in the banks' practice of taking references and making enquiries about a new customer, and attributes this partly to the increased protection to the banks when collecting cheques provided by the Cheques Act 1957 (we shall also examine this in Chapter 6) and to the enormous increase in the number of people seeking to open bank accounts, with the resulting competitive pressures on banks. Reference is made to relaxed practices of banks in other countries also, but says that the UK must set its own standards. It concludes that the banks must initiate procedures which allow them to establish, to their reasonable satisfaction, the identity of a person opening an account, so that if subsequently challenged, they would be able to refer to the action they took at the time.

If you are employed in a bank examine your own bank's policy with regard to taking up references in respect of new customers and discuss with your colleagues the extent to which policy may have changed in recent years.

Closing an account

As we saw in Chapter 4 (see p. 61) banks must be careful to give adequate notice to a customer when the bank decides to close his account. No precise period of notice is given in either case law or statute law, but it is reasonable to assume that for a personal account 1 month would be satisfactory. Obviously a bank will not want to close an account unless it has been run in an unsatisfactory manner – for example, where the customer has frequently drawn cheques for which there are insufficient funds, or uncleared funds, on the account and the bank has been obliged to return such cheques unpaid. This is only likely to happen, of course, where the customer's financial position is weak – if he were financially sound the bank would most likely allow an overdraft, even if arrangements for it had not been made in advance, especially if the customer had securities lodged with the bank.

Types of personal account holder

Married women   A married woman can own property in the same way as if she were unmarried, and she can enter into any contract and be sued for a debt or a tort. She is also subject to the law of bankruptcy as if she were a single person. A married woman may therefore open and run an account, borrow money and pledge security to the bank and avail herself of all the other banking services. However, if she is a minor the rules for opening and running an account for a minor will of course apply (see below).

Despite the Sex Discrimination Act 1975, some banks still require to know the name of a married woman's husband, his employer's name and his occupation, when opening an account for her. This is because of the decision in *Savory and Co.* v. *Lloyds Bank Ltd* (1932), in which the bank was found negligent in not finding out these details when opening a wife's account. Quite apart from this, the bank will want the usual references. When a married woman deposits security on behalf of another person banks usually arrange for her to be independently advised by a solicitor. This is particularly desirable where she is lodging security in respect of her husband's account.

Many married women have no income of their own apart from interest and dividends on their investments, and may therefore be in the position of being able to claim tax relief on such receipts up to their personal income tax allowance. An interest-bearing account is therefore likely to be suitable to a married woman, for if she obtains a certificate from the Inland Revenue and supplies it to the bank the interest can be paid without deduction of tax.

Minors   A minor is a person under 18 years of age, and as such is not normally bound by contracts apart from those in respect of necessities, such as food. He or she cannot give a guarantee, but can borrow against the guarantee of an adult. Minors can assume liability for contracts made before 18 years of age, once they have reached that age (Minors' Contracts Act 1987).

When opening an account for a young person, the banker must endeavour to ascertain his or her age, and record the date of the 18th birthday. Normally the account should be kept in credit, but bankers do frequently use their discretion in allowing a small overdraft, even though legally they have no claim for repayment. The general practice these days is to provide a minor over 16 with a current account and a cheque book, but cheque guarantee cards and ATM cards are issued only where circumstances permit, e.g. a family connection. It is also common practice for savings accounts to be offered to children under 16, but where the account holder is under 7 the account has to be operated by a parent. Some banks allow ATM cards to be held by youngsters over 13, provided a parent gives permission in writing.

Credit cards are not issued to minors as it is an offence under the Consumer Credit Act 1974 to grant credit within the terms of the Act to a minor. Debit cards can be supplied provided they do not permit credit to the holder.

A minor may be a partner, and can operate on a partnership account and even incur an overdraft, as agent for the partnership. He is not personally liable, however, until he reaches the 18th birthday, except for his own share of the partnership assets in the event of bankruptcy of the partnership.

Similarly, a minor may be a party to a joint account but would not be liable for any overdraft on the account before he reached 18 years of age.

Joint accounts   When an account is opened in the names of two or more persons, the bank requires its standard form of mandate to be signed. This must indicate whether one, or some, or all of the parties are to sign on the account and to withdraw items of security from the bank.

Even though not all of the parties need to sign on the account to make withdrawals, the mandate will establish that they are all liable in respect of any money borrowed from the bank. This liability is always **joint and several**, i.e. there is a right of action against all the parties to the account jointly, and then on an individual basis against each party until the whole debt is recovered. There is a right of set-off between the private accounts of the individual parties and their joint account, and death does not release the estate of a deceased party for debts owing on the joint account.

When one of the parties to a joint account dies, the bank would by common law obtain a good discharge by paying over a credit balance to the surviving parties or by taking a new mandate on the account signed by the surviving parties. The rule of survivorship must apply, but this becomes a matter for the surviving parties to sort out for themselves, provided that the bank's mandate establishes quite clearly that the intention of the parties was that upon the death of one of them the balance should be vested in the survivors. Safe custodies are usually handed over against the signatures of the surviving parties to the account and of the personal representatives of the deceased party.

The bankruptcy of one party cancels the mandate, and the account must be stopped and the credit balance released on the signatures of the solvent party(ies) and the trustee or official receiver. If there is an overdraft, the bankrupt's security will be released only if the remaining parties repay the overdraft or undertake (with the bank's approval) to do so. Safe custodies will be released on the joint authority of the remaining parties and the trustee or official receiver.

Mental incapacity (see below) also determines the mandate on a joint account, and the account must be stopped. A credit balance can be released against the signatures of the remaining parties and the Court of Protection. The incapacitated party's securities against an overdraft will be released only if the other parties to the account repay the overdraft, and safe custodies will be released against joint signatures in the same way as a credit balance.

Where the bank becomes aware of serious disagreement between the parties to a joint account, for example between husband and wife who are contemplating divorce, it may be wise to insist that all parties to the account sign cheques on the account even though the mandate stipulates that only one signature will suffice.

Personal representatives   The personal representatives of a deceased person are executors if there is a will, or administrators if there is not. Executors are appointed in the will, administrators are appointed by the court. Where executors refuse to act (or are incapable of acting) administrators may be appointed.

An executor's powers to act are confirmed by **probate**, which is an official copy of the will with a certificate that the will has been proved. Letters of administration are granted to the administrator(s). These documents must be presented by the personal representative(s) before a credit balance and securities and safe custodies of the deceased can be withdrawn. If the account is overdrawn, the personal representatives may choose to pay off the overdraft in order to obtain release of securities, or to sell off the securities for the purpose of repaying the overdraft.

If executors or administrators are unknown, the usual references must be obtained before opening an account for them. The account is opened in the names of the executors or administrators, with an indication in the title of the account that they are executors or administrators of the deceased. The mandate indicates whether one or all of the personal representatives are to sign, and always establishes joint and several liability in respect of the advance. As inheritance tax has to be paid before probate or letters of administration can be obtained personal representatives very frequently require bank finance to enable the tax to be paid.

Mental incapacity   If it is known that a customer's mental condition is such that he cannot manage his own affairs it will be necessary for the relatives to apply to the Court of Protection to appoint someone to act as receiver to handle his affairs, within the provisions of the Mental Health Act 1983. If, however, the customer, when mentally fit, had signed an enduring power of attorney, the person appointed in that deed is able to continue handling the affairs of the signatory to the deed even though he has become mentally incapable of doing so himself.

Club and society accounts   These have been included under personal accounts because such bodies are unincorporated associations which have no separate entity legally, and therefore cannot be sued in their own name. Furthermore, the officers are private individuals who run the small accounts for their associations with very limited formality. They are non-profit making associations, and as such are not partnerships. The members are not liable in respect of any borrowing by the club or society unless they have given their own personal assent.

When the account is opened, the bank requires its appropriate mandate form to be signed which confirms that a meeting of the association resolved that the account should be opened and that certain officers should sign on the account. Usually the mandate bears the signature of the chairman or president as well as those of the persons to sign on the account. A copy of the society's rules will also be required.

Borrowing is not usually involved and, if it is, should be allowed only if the association's rules permit. Security should be taken if at all possible, such as a guarantee of one (or some) of the members.

5.3   Business Accounts

Sole traders

Where an individual trades in his own name he is known as a sole trader, even though he may have a number of employees. He is personally liable for all the debts of the business and this means that some or all of his personal assets, including his house, may have to be sold to meet the debts of the business. This is a disadvantage compared with a partnership or a company where others share responsibility for the business, and with a limited company where possibly many share in that responsibility but the liability is limited to the amount of the shares held.

Sole traders do not have to publish accounts (though they may have to produce accounts for tax purposes), and consequently suppliers may be reluctant to grant them credit. Since the Finance Act 1993 small businesses with a turnover of less than £15,000 do not have to produce detailed accounts to the Inland Revenue but simply the amount of profit or loss.

The sole trader has the advantages of being his own boss and not having to go through the formalities of meetings with partners and not having to draw up published accounts. However, he is on his own and this can be a problem should he fall ill. He also has the advantage, compared with an employee, of being able to claim the expenses of running the business against his income from the business in being assessed for tax purposes. For instance, if he is working from home, a proportion of the heating, lighting and telephone expenses could be offset against his income.

As far as opening the account is concerned, the sole trader is treated as a normal personal account holder, but it is necessary to record any business name that he may use, for instance, John Smith trading as Court Shoes. Normally sole traders keep a separate account for the business so as to keep the business affairs quite separate from their private accounts.

Partnership accounts

The Partnership Act 1890 defines a partnership as 'the relation which subsists between persons carrying on business in common with a view of profit'. There need be no written agreement or deed between the partners, it can be simply a verbal or implied agreement. There must be not more than 20 partners, except where the partnership consists of practising solicitors or accountants or persons carrying on business as members of the Stock Exchange.

A partnership has no separate entity (except in Scotland) and therefore any action against the partnership must be taken against the **partners themselves**. All partners are responsible for the firm's debts, and may be made bankrupt to pay for them. It is no longer necessary for a firm carrying on business under a business name to register that name with the Registrar of Business Names; all that is required is that the names of all the partners appear on business notepaper, circulars, etc. and for the names and addresses of the partners to be displayed.

In opening an account for a partnership, a banker cannot therefore rely on a certificate of registration for confirmation of the names of the partners and may need to see the firm's notepaper or other business documents for confirmation, or visit the premises. A banker must be cautious at the outset because the bank will doubtlessly be collecting cheques payable to the firm and could conceivably be sued for conversion should they be paid into a bogus account in the firm's name by persons who pretended to be true owners of the firm.

Every partner is an agent of the firm unless the partnership agreement provides to the contrary, and binds the partnership unless the person dealing with the partner concerned is aware of his lack of authority. In a trading firm (one involved in buying and selling goods) there is an implied authority for any partner to bind the firm in respect of bills of exchange (including cheques), promissory notes, contracts of borrowings, and a pledge or sale of the firm's assets except on transactions under seal. In a non-trading firm, a partner cannot bind the firm in respect of these items apart from cheques unless they are part of the firm's usual business. A partner cannot without express authority bind a firm by deed nor execute a guarantee in the firm's name, unless giving guarantees forms part of a firm's usual business. All partners must therefore normally be involved in signing a guarantee.

When opening an account for a partnership, the banker will require a mandate signed by all the partners which covers the drawing of cheques and borrowing and charging of securities, and will include a clause in which the partners accept joint and several liability. Signatures on the account may be in the name of the firm or on behalf of the firm.

When collecting cheques for a partner's private account drawn on the partnership, the bank is not put on enquiry unless the cheques are exceptionally large or there is some doubt about the partner's integrity. However, a bank is put on enquiry when cheques payable to the partnership are paid into a partner's account, and likewise if cheques are drawn by the partnership and payable to third parties and indorsed.

Upon the death of a partner, an account that is in credit may be continued by the remaining partners in order to wind up the business, but a new mandate is required. If there is a debit balance it is desirable to claim against the deceased's estate and for this reason the account should be stopped.

Partnerships are easy to set up and have the advantage, compared with sole trading, of having several partners who may be able to provide additional capital if necessary. Furthermore, the responsibilities can be shared out and the partners can cover for each other in the event of sickness or other absences. However no one partner is his own boss and disagreements may easily arise between partners, especially over the unwise actions of one partner for which all the partners are liable. There may also be a problem upon the death or retirement of a partner as it may be necessary to buy out that partner.

Company accounts

A company is a corporation – i.e., a legal person which by law exists and has rights and duties quite separate and distinct from the members of the cor- poration. Apart from companies set up by Royal Charter and nationalised cor- porations established by Act of Parliament, the majority of commercial companies are set up by registration under the Companies Acts. They are incorporated by registering specified documents with the Registrar of Com- panies. Such registration as a company is also available to non-commercial organisations such as charities.

Companies may be **unlimited**, which means that in the event of insolvency the members are liable for the company's debts without limit and their own personal assets may have to be used in settling the company's debts. Alter- natively, the company may be **limited by shares or by guarantee** and as such is usually formed for non-trading purposes such as a university or col- lege. In the first of these two types of limited company the liability of the members of the company is limited to the amount of their shareholdings, and this is the situation with the vast majority of companies. In the second type, the liability of each individual member is limited to the amount of the guar- antee which he has given to the company. Companies also fit into one of two other categories, public companies and private companies. A public company may offer its shares and debentures to the general public, but a private com- pany may not. Both types of company must have at least two members but there is no upper limit on the number of members (although private com- panies tend still to restrict the size of membership and to restrict the transfer of their shares).

Whether a company is public or private the procedure for incorporation is the same. 5 documents must be registered with the Registrar of Companies:

1 Memorandum of Association
2 Articles of Association
3 A statement giving the names of the directors and of the secretary, and accompanied by their written consents to be directors; included in the statement must be the address of the registered office

4   A declaration of compliance with the Companies Act 1948 concerning registration
5   A statement of the company's capital, if there is any

Of these documents, the first two are particularly important and need to be examined in detail.

The **Memorandum of Association** is the company's charter with the outside world, and the company can act only within the powers laid down in it. The memorandum contains the name and registered office of the company. The name must end with the word Limited (Ltd) if it is a private company, and Public Limited Company (plc) if it is a public company (or Welsh equivalents). In addition, the objects of the company must be given, the company's powers, the fact that liability is to be limited, and the authorised capital of the company.

The objects clause must give details of the purposes for which the company has been formed. If any transaction entered into by the company after its incorporation exceeds those authorised in the objects clause, it may be *ultra vires* (beyond the powers) and such an act cannot be rectified by members of the company. However, the European Communities Act 1972 provides that anyone dealing with a company can enforce an *ultra vires* contract against it if he dealt in good faith and if the transaction was decided on by the directors. The same Act stipulated that a third party may assume that the powers of directors to bind the company are not limited under the memorandum and articles of association, that he need not enquire as to the capacity of the company to enter into the transaction or about the powers of the directors. He is presumed to have acted in good faith unless it can be proved that the contrary is the case. However, it is doubtful whether a bank could claim protection under these provisions in that it would receive a copy of the memorandum and articles when the account was opened. The company's powers – such as to borrow money and acquire businesses – will usually be listed in addition to its objects.

The **Articles of Association** are concerned with the relationship between the company and its members. They are concerned, for instance, with the rights of shareholders to vote at the company's meetings, the issue and transfer of shares, the powers of directors and the conduct of meetings.

The memorandum and articles of association are both public documents, and may be inspected at the office of the Registrar of Companies.

When the Registrar of Companies is satisfied with the documents filed with it, he issues a **certificate of incorporation** which brings the company into existence. A private company may then commence business, but a public company must not do so (nor borrow any money) until it has been issued with a certificate that the share capital requirements have been complied with. This certificate is called a **trading certificate**. A public company will also need to seek permission from the Stock Exchange Council to be listed on the Stock Exchange or to be placed on the Unlisted Securities Market (USM) which is run by the Stock Exchange.

When opening an account for a limited company, the bank will need to see the certificate of incorporation. If the company is a public company, it may open an account for the receipt of capital subscriptions only, pending the receipt of the trading certificate. The bank will also require, for both types of company, a certified copy of the resolution appointing the first directors of the company, unless they are named in the articles of association. The bank's mandate form will also need to be signed by the chairman and secretary of the company after a meeting of the board of directors has been held passing the resolution contained in the mandate form. This mandate will include the names and signatures of those persons who may sign on the account. Anyone signing cheques and other instruments on behalf of the company must sign 'per pro' or 'for and on behalf of', indicating the name of the company and, after the signature, the capacity in the company – i.e. secretary or director.

The bank must examine the company's memorandum and articles of association and be satisfied that the company's activities are generally in conformity with them. If the company is to borrow money, the bank must examine the memorandum to see if it is specific about borrowing money, and also the articles to see if the directors' powers are limited.

The main advantage of a limited company compared with sole trading and partnership is that the liability of the member is limited to the amount of his shareholding or guarantee. There is also the advantage that the shareholding may be sold so that there is no continuity problem if a shareholder dies as there would be with a sole proprietorship or a partnership. Furthermore, a company of reasonable size may be better able to employ good specialist managers.

Against these advantages must be offset the complex nature of the legal requirements for setting up the company, the formalities involved in running it, and the fact that the company's accounts have to be submitted to the Registrar of Companies and are available for inspection by the general public.

5.4 The Rule in *Clayton's Case*

In order to protect the bank's interest it is sometimes necessary to break an account so as to establish the balance as at a particular date. A new account is opened, carrying forward the old balance. The reason for this action is the so-called Rule in *Clayton's Case*, dating back to 1816, a ruling of considerable importance to bankers. The Rule is that payments into a current account are appropriated to the debit items in order of date, unless it can be shown that either the customer or the bank clearly appropriates particular credits for the payment of particular debits. An illustration will make this rule more easily understood:

Account of Peter Jones

	Debit £	Credit £	Balance £
February 10	500		Dr 500
February 15	300		Dr 800
February 20	200		Dr 1,000
March 1		700	Dr 300
March 4		200	Dr 100

According to the Rule the payments in on March 1 and 4 will have nearly extinguished the three debits in February and leave an overdrawn balance of £100. But if something happened during the period February 20–March 1 which would cause the bank to need to establish the debt at £1,000 they could have broken the account and, despite the two payments in during March, make a claim for that amount. For example, if a partnership ceased on February 21 because of the death of a partner, the bank would need to make a claim against the partner's estate for the outstanding debt of £1,000. By breaking the account at that date it could resist any claim that the subsequent payments in were meant to pay off virtually all of the debits, and that the claim against the estate should be only £100. Similarly if Peter Jones' overdraft was supported by a guarantee from a third party and, because his account had not been run in a satisfactory manner, the bank decided to call in that guarantee on February 21, it could establish the debt at £1,000 by breaking the account and notifying the guarantor that day of the amount it was claiming against the guarantee. The guarantor could not then claim that the later payments reduced his liability under the Rule in *Clayton's Case*.

There are many instances in which the Rule in *Clayton's Case* could be to the bank's disadvantage and therefore it is wise to break an account to avoid this, but it is not necessary for us to examine them in detail at this stage. When you go on to the Associateship examinations of the Chartered Institute of Bankers you will see just how very important the Rule is.

It is important to note that a customer is at liberty to specify, when he pays in money, a particular cheque(s) that is to be paid with it and this prevents the Rule in *Clayton's Case* from operating. Similarly, when a credit is paid in and the customer does not specify a particular payment out in this way, the bank could notify him that it is keeping the funds to make a particular payment out of the account.

Review Questions

1   Which personal details are certain to be included in the application form when an individual opens an account? (5.2)
2   Why are specimen signatures necessary? (5.2)
3   How might a bank identify a would-be customer who is new to the bank? (5.2)
4   Why does a bank have to be so cautious when opening an account for a stranger? (5.2)
5   Why is it important to glean as much information as possible about a potential customer's financial status when opening the account? (5.2)
6   Why would it be wise for a bank to take up references if a stranger wishes to open an account? Do banks always take up references? (5.2)
7   In what law case was a bank successfully sued for not taking up references when opening an account? (5.2)
8   In what two cases did banks take up references but were nevertheless subsequently sued for negligence? (5.2)
9   What did the Jack Committee have to say about the failure of banks to take up references? (5.2)
10   May married women be offered normal banking facilities? In what circumstances might a married woman be treated differently from a single woman or from a man? (5.2)
11   May a minor overdraw his/her account? (5.2)
12   May a credit card be issued to a minor? (5.2)
13   What is meant by joint and several liability? (5.2)
14   What happens to a joint account when one of the parties to it dies? (5.2)
15   What happens to a joint account when one of the parties to it is declared bankrupt? (5.2)
16   What happens to a joint account when one of the parties to it becomes mentally incapable? (5.2)
17   Can a bank insist that both or all of the parties to a joint account sign cheques, even though the mandate states that only one signature is necessary? (5.2)
18   What is meant by the term personal representative? (5.2)
19   Might a bank lend money to the executors of a will in order to pay inheritance tax? (5.2)
20   Why should a bank obtain a copy of a club's rules before opening an account for it? (5.2)
21   What are the advantages and disadvantages of being a sole trader compared to being a member of a partnership? (5.3)
22   How would you define a partnership? (5.3)
23   Why is joint and several liability so important in connection with partnership accounts? (5.3)
24   Do partnerships have to be registered? (5.3)

Review Questions   cont'd.

25   Is a bank put on enquiry when collecting cheques for a partner's private account drawn on the partnership or payable to the partnership? (5.3)

26   What is meant by a corporation? (5.3)

27   How would you distinguish between a company limited by shares and one limited by guarantee? (5.3)

28   How would you distinguish between private companies and public companies? (5.3)

29   What is the minimum number of shareholders in a company? Is there a maximum number? (5.3)

30   Which 5 documents have to be registered by a new company with the Registrar of Companies? (5.3)

31   What is a memorandum of association, and what facts must it contain? (5.3)

32   What is meant by the term *ultra vires*? (5.3)

33   What are articles of association? (5.3)

34   What is a certificate of incorporation? Can a public company commence business as soon as it receives this document? (5.3)

35   Summarise the details that must be contained in a bank's mandate form for a company account. (5.3)

36   Why is it important for a bank to examine a customer company's memorandum and articles of association? (5.3)

37   What are the advantages and disadvantages of trading as a company rather than a partnership? (5.3)

38   What is the Rule in Clayton's Case? Explain its importance for the banker. (5.4)

Past Examination Questions

1   Explain briefly why the banker, when opening an account, should:
    (a) obtain references for a personal account   (*6 marks*)

    (b) know the names of all the individuals in a partnership   (*6 marks*)

    (c) examine the Memorandum and Articles of Association for a
         company account.   (*8 marks*)

2   Outline the banking considerations and legal formalities which apply to
    opening the following accounts:
    (a) Jane and John Dough want to open an account where they can each
         pay in or draw out money.   (*12 marks*)

    (b) Eddie Kenieval is aged 16. He wants an account which would
         allow him to borrow money to buy a motorcycle. He also wants a
         credit card.   (*5 marks*)

    (c) Mrs M. Roofmender wants an account of her own. Her husband is
         an accountant and gives her an allowance for work she does for
         him. She does not pay tax.   (*3 marks*)

3   (a) Businesses can operate as sole traders, partnerships or limited
         companies. List the main advantages and disadvantages of each
         business type in note, chart or tabular form.   (*14 marks*)

    (b) Give one factor, requirement or consideration that the banker will
         think about when opening or operating an account for each
         business type mentioned in (a).   (*6 marks*)

6 The use of cheques

Chapter objectives

When you have carefully studied this chapter you should be able to:
- Define a cheque and draw a specimen cheque
- Explain the various types of crossings on a cheque and their significance
- Explain what is meant by the term endorsement and define the different types of endorsements
- Discuss in detail the roles of the collecting and paying bankers

6.1   Introduction

In this chapter we will examine the cheques system in detail and the roles of the collecting and paying bankers. It is necessary to know the legal definition of a cheque, and to arrive at this we have to examine the definition of a bill of exchange, because a cheque is in fact a bill of exchange.

It is essential that the practising banker should know the significance of a crossing on a cheque, and of the various types of crossings, and why some cheques have to be endorsed.

The roles of the collecting and paying bankers are very important in view of the possible consequences to the banker if he acts negligently in collecting or paying a cheque. These roles will therefore be dealt with in some detail in this chapter.

6.2   Bills of Exchange

Before we can define a cheque it is necessary for us to define a bill of exchange and to examine its functions, because a cheque is itself a bill of exchange – a rather special type of bill of exchange, as we shall see (see Figure 6.1).

Up to the middle of the nineteenth century when the cheque came into its own the main method of settling debts was to use a bill of exchange, and as far as international trade is concerned it is still a main method of payment. Bills were at first a device which enabled debts to be married up against one another, but with

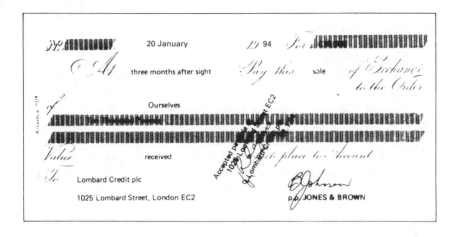

Figure 6.1 Inland bill of exchange

the development of the international banking system bills of exchange are seldom used in this way now, and instead each transaction is settled on its own. Merchants married up debts by offsetting debts due to residents abroad for goods imported into Britain, for instance, against payments due to British exporters. If someone in Italy who had a payment to make to a merchant in Britain accepted a usance bill for, say, 90 days drawn on him by the merchant, he had that period of time in which to find an Italian exporter(s) who had a bill(s) which had been accepted by an importer in Britain. If he bought this bill for Italian lire he could then send it to an agent in Britain with a request that he presented it for payment in sterling and used the proceeds to pay his own bill when due.

Today the use of agents in this way is no longer necessary, and instead the bills of exchange and shipping documents (if any) to which they relate are sent through the banking system which collects bills on the instructions of its customers. In addition, the banks provide finance for exporters in anticipation of the proceeds of bills by discounting them, i.e. buying them at their face value less discount. In the case of foreign bills this process is referred to as **negotiating** a bill, and involves more than the simple purchase of the bill in that the shipping documents are also delivered by the banking system to the overseas buyer.

Let us look at the inland bill of exchange illustrated in Figure 6.1.

The bill has been drawn by Jones & Brown (the drawer) on Lombard Credit plc (the drawee), possibly as a means of obtaining temporary accommodation. The payee is Jones & Brown because they have made the bill payable to the 'Order of ourselves'. The bill has been accepted by Lombard Credit plc, who are thus the acceptor of the bill. It is payable on 20 April 1994, which is 90 days after date.

What are the advantages to the parties concerned of using this method of settlement? Firstly, the bill is evidence of a debt and as it has been accepted it is legally enforceable against Lombard Credit plc. Secondly, it allows the drawee a period of time in which to make the payment, and lastly the drawer, if he requires it, can obtain immediate finance. The provision of this finance cannot be forced upon anyone, of course, and if the bill had been drawn upon some unknown small firm Jones & Brown might have had difficulty in getting it discounted. Obviously this would not be so with Lombard Credit plc for we can assume that it is a well-known London merchant bank. If the market rate for bank bills (bills drawn on and accepted by banks) is 10 per cent, then Jones & Brown will receive approximately £9,750 (£10,000 less interest for roughly 3 months at 10 per cent). The institution buying the bill can then either hold it until maturity or resell (rediscount) it, and it will be presented for payment to Lombard Credit on 20 April by the then holder.

If after having had the bill accepted Jones & Brown decide not to discount it but use it as a means of paying a debt to some other firm, then they will simply endorse the bill in blank, i.e. simply sign their name on the back. They could alternatively specially endorse it over to another party by writing on the back of the bill an instruction to pay that party and signing their name under that instruction. Jones & Brown will be the endorser and the other party is the endorsee.

Having examined how a bill of exchange is used and the advantages of so doing, we are now in a position to look at the official definition of a bill of exchange. This is to be found in the Bills of Exchange Act 1882 as:

> An unconditional order in writing, addressed by one person to another, signed by the person giving it, requiring the person to whom it is addressed to pay on demand or at a fixed or determinable future time a sum certain in money to, or to the order of, a specified person, or to bearer.

Referring to our sample bill in Figure 6.1, the bill is addressed by Jones & Brown to Lombard Credit plc. These are both persons because in the legal sense the word 'person' includes not only an individual or partnership of people but any company or institution which is a **legal person**. It is signed by Jones & Brown and it requires the person to whom it is addressed (Lombard Credit plc) to pay at a determinable future time (3 months after receiving the bill for acceptance), a fixed sum of money (£10,000). It is payable to the order of a specified person (Jones & Brown).

We can now relate this definition of a bill of exchange to a cheque which is a special form of bill.

6.3   Cheques

Definition

According to the Bills of Exchange Act 1882 a cheque is a bill of exchange drawn on a banker payable on demand. We can therefore use the definition of a bill of exchange (see above) in defining a cheque. All of that definition applies except that 'the person to whom it is addressed' must be a bank and the words 'or at a fixed or determinable future time' must be deleted.

From this definition, it is clear that a cheque must not be conditional. Therefore a cheque which includes a clause such as 'provided that I find the car in good working order' would not be legally valid. Such a clause would of course put an unbearable restraint upon a banker paying a cheque, for he could hardly be expected to have to check on whether the drawer was satisfied before he made the payment. A cheque which includes a receipt form and an instruction that it must be signed is nevertheless unconditional provided that the instruction is not made an essential requirement for payment by the bank.

A cheque must be in writing, and this term includes typewriting and printing. The essential point is that it must not be only a verbal instruction. The Act does not say that it must be written on paper, and therefore cheques which have been chiselled into stone, or even written on the back of a cow, presumably with a branding iron, have been presented (and paid by banks) (see Figure 6.2)!

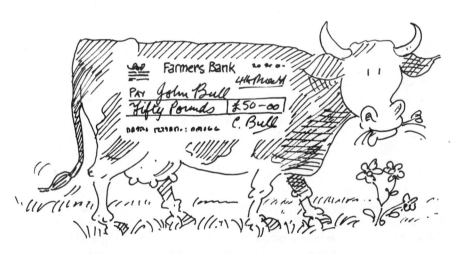

Figure 6.2   'An unconditional order in writing ...'

Development of the cheque system

The cheque first came into use in the seventeenth century but did not really come into its own until well into the nineteenth century with the establishment of the joint stock banks and their networks of branches. The increased use of banks by the public led to the recognition of the cheque as a convenient (and safe) means of settlement. In the twentieth century, increasing affluence, especially after the Second World War, extended the use of bank accounts to people who previously did not feel the need to have them, and the Wages Act 1960 (which legalised the payment of wages by cheque) encouraged this development. The introduction of cheque guarantee cards has enabled shopkeepers and other traders to accept cheques without fear of loss, making the cheque an even more convenient means of payment. Bank service till cards which enable account holders to obtain cash at times when the banks are closed, have encouraged the opening of current accounts, and with them the further use of cheques. Another development which encouraged the use of cheques was the abolition of the stamp duty on cheques in 1971.

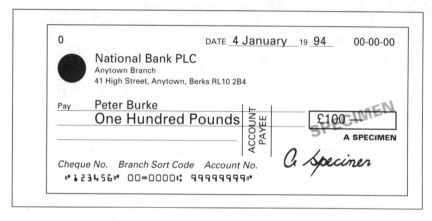

Figure 6.3   Specimen cheque

A specimen cheque   An example of a cheque is given in Figure 6.3. The **drawer** of the cheque is A. Specimen who has given the bank (National in this instance) an instruction to pay £100 to Peter Burke. National Bank is the **drawee** of the cheque and Peter Burke is the **payee**. The cheque is crossed 'Account Payee' (a term which we shall look at later on in this chapter), and is in line with the majority of cheques now drawn. As we shall see on page 95, the Bills of Exchange Act 1882 was amended in 1992 with the intention of limiting the transfer of cheques from person to person. This was achieved by legally recognising the crossing 'Account Payee' and stating specifically that a cheque bearing this crossing is not transferable. A collecting banker who permits a cheque that has been crossed this way to be paid into an account other than that of the payee does so at his own risk.

If the drawer of a cheque wants to make it possible for the payee to transfer the ownership of the cheque to some other person, then he must delete the 'Account Payee' crossing and sign or initial the alteration. Alernatively, if he wishess to issue a number of these cheques, he should ask his bank for a cheque book in which the cheques have not been crossed in this way. If this specimen chequee had been of the transferable type, Peter Burke could have specially endorsed the cheque over to a third party by writing on the back, for example, 'Pay Paul

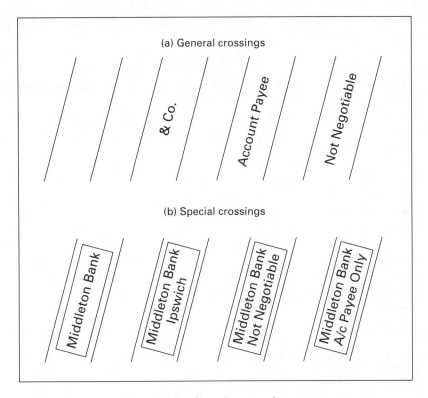

Figure 6.4   Crossings on cheques

Conrad' and signing under this instruction. Peter Burke would then be the **endorser** of the cheque and Paul Conrad the **endorsee**. Alternatively, he could have simply endorsed it in blank, i.e. signed his name on the back of the cheque and the next holder would have to add his endorsement before paying it into his account or passing the cheque on to another person.

Crossings on cheques (see Figure 6.4)

By crossing a cheque the drawer greatly increases the protection afforded by the Bills of Exchange Act, in that the cheque can be paid only to a banker. This means that the holder must pay it in to an account so that the bank will obtain payment for it, and the holder cannot obtain payment for it in cash at a bank counter. If therefore a crossed cheque is stolen the thief cannot obtain cash for it, and if he or she pays it into an account he or she may be traced. The thief may of course, transfer title to the cheque to some other person who pays it into an account having taken the cheque in good faith and for value. Provided he or she had no knowledge of the defect of title, this transferee may claim to be a holder in due course (see below).

The Bills of Exchange Act (in s.79(2)) stipulates that:

> Where a banker on whom a cheque is drawn ... pays a cheque crossed generally otherwise than to a banker, or if crossed specially otherwise than to the banker to whom it is crossed, or his agent for collecting being a banker, he is liable to the true owner of the cheque for any loss he may sustain owing to the cheque having been so paid.

General crossing   A general crossing involves drawing two parallel transverse lines across the face of a cheque. Sometimes the words 'and company' (or an abbreviation, & Co.) are added between the lines, but this practice is seldom adopted today: it is a relic of the past when banks were private companies. Also (or instead) if he wishes, the drawer may write the words 'Not Negotiable' between the lines, and this, as we shall see, means that anyone who takes the cheque cannot receive a better title to it than that of the person transferring it. The addition of these words does not make the crossing a special one, and it is still a general crossing.

Special crossing   A cheque is crossed specially when the name of a particular bank is written across the face of a cheque, with or without two parallel transverse lines. The words 'not negotiable' may be added to this crossing. As we can see from the wording of s.79(2) above, the significance of a special crossing is that the cheque can be paid only to the banker named in the crossing or through another bank which is acting as its agent. A special crossing thus gives added protection.

Who may cross a cheque?   The Bills of Exchange Act stipulates who has authority to cross a cheque:

1 A cheque may be crossed generally or specially by the drawer
2 Where a cheque is uncrossed, the holder may cross it generally or specially
3 Where a cheque is crossed generally, the holder may cross it specially
4 Where a cheque is crossed generally or specially, the holder may add the words 'not negotiable'
5 Where a cheque is crossed specially, the banker to whom it is crossed may again cross it specially to another banker for collection
6 Where an uncrossed cheque, or a cheque crossed generally, is sent to a banker for collection, the banker may also cross it specially to the bank itself

The important thing to remember about crossed cheques is that they are not encashable at a bank counter. Most cheque books contain crossed cheques these days and the words 'Account Payee' also appear in the crossing (we shall look at the significance of these words shortly). As we have seen, it is much safer for the customer to use crossed cheques which can be traced to the account into which they are paid. When a bank customer wants to cash a cheque at his bank, he is usually allowed to use his crossed cheques for the purpose these days whereas until recently it was quite common to require him or her to 'open' the crossing by writing 'Pay Cash' through the crossing and adding his signature. It is strictly speaking contrary to the law for a bank to cash a crossed cheque, but obviously a bank runs little risk in paying cash to its own customer against such an instrument.

Account Payee crossings

The Jack Report examined the various types of crossing on cheques and felt that it was necessary to streamline these in order to simplify the task of the paying banker and to remove the confusion which surrounds crossings on cheques. The Committee even went so far as to recommend that a new type of instrument should be introduced which could not be transferred by the payee and which would be easily recognised as a bank payment order and not a cheque. There would also be less risk attached to this new instrument. Cheques could still be used if a transferable instrument was required.

The government did not take up the suggestion of a new type of instrument but, instead, amended the law by the Cheques Act 1992 which gave legal backing to the concept of non-transferable cheques by recognising the Account Payee crossing that until then had no statutory significance. The 1992 Act adds a new section (s.81A) to the Bills of Exchange Act 1882 as follows:

(1) Where a cheque is crossed and bears across its face the words 'account payee' or 'a/c payee', either with or without the word 'only', the cheque shall not be transferable, but shall only be valid as between the parties thereto.

(2) A banker is not to be treated for the purposes of section 80 [of the Bills of Exchange Act] as having been negligent by reason only of his failure to concern himself with any purported endorsement of a cheque which under subsection (1) above or otherwise is not transferable.

We shall be examining the second part of this new section later in this chapter when we consider the responsibilities of the collecting and paying bankers; for now we are concerned with the first part. The banks now issue cheque books to their private account customers with the 'Account Payee' crossing printed on them and only if a customer specifically asks for a book of cheques without this crossing or with no crossing at all will he or she receive such a cheque book. The banks have pointed out to their customers that Account Payee cheques cannot be signed on the back and given to someone else to be paid into their bank account. This new standard cheque offers a higher level of security against fraud, but it does of course make it difficult for the person without an account to get payment for a cheque.

The words 'not transferable' have on occasions been used in the past as an alternative to 'account payee' and, although they too have not had any legal backing, they served as a warning to a collecting bank not to allow the cheque concerned to be paid into the account of anyone other than the payee. Clearly a banker who allowed this to happen was in danger of being charged with negligence should the cheque have been misappropriated. With the introduction of the new style of standard cheque the 'not transferable' crossing would add nothing to the cheque and will presumably fall completely out of use.

The concept of negotiability

A cheque is a negotiable instrument and so too are other bills of exchange, and such instruments as promissory notes, dividend warrants, bearer debentures and Treasury bills.

The full legal title to a negotiable instrument is transferred by delivery (or by endorsement and delivery) to the person receiving it, provided that he or she has a good title to it, even if a previous holder had a bad title. The recipient must be acting in good faith, and be unaware that a previous holder's title was a bad one. This puts a negotiable instrument in a rather different category from an article – because if someone bought a car, for instance, in good faith and not knowing it had been stolen before it was sold, the rightful owner could repossess it. The purchaser would have to endeavour to get his or her money back from the vendor, and if he was unsuccessful he or she would have to bear the loss.

If I receive a cheque payable to me which is not marked 'Account Payee' and I endorse it and leave it about, then I do so at my own risk because, if it is stolen and fraudulently passed on by the thief to someone in settlement of a debt, I would have no redress against that person. He could pay the cheque into a bank account, and thus receive value for it, provided that he had taken it from the thief, or some subsequent holder, in good faith and without any reason to suspect that the thief's title was not good.

This concept of negotiability will now be of much less significance given that the majority of personal cheques will have the Account Payee crossing printed on them, thus restricting the number of parties to a cheque. They will no longer be transferable and therefore a previous holder(s) will not be involved when a cheque is paid to, say, a retailer in payment for goods. The retailer must simply satisfy himself about the status of his customer, the drawer of the cheque, and if the customer supports the cheque with a bank guarantee card that covers the amount of the goods, all well and good.

Endorsements on cheques

We briefly looked at the subject of endorsements earlier in this chapter (p. 90, 92), and it is now necessary to consider the subject in the light of the Cheques Act

1957. The main purpose of this Act was to abolish the need for endorsements, which in fact it did. However, the Act went much further than the banks wanted and, in consequence, they issued a notice to the public saying that they would still require endorsements on some cheques, on other bills of exchange, and on travellers' cheques and promissory notes. The effect of this notice was that only cheques paid in by the payee to his own account need no longer be endorsed and, as the vast majority of cheques are of this type, the practice of the banks of checking for endorsements was greatly reduced. Instead of turning over every cheque paid in to see that it was endorsed and, also, that it was correctly endorsed, the cashier simply looks at the front of each cheque to ensure that it is payable to the account holder and turns over only those that are payable to a third party.

The Cheques Act also did away with the habit of asking for a receipt when paying by cheque, because it provides that 'an unendorsed cheque which appears to have been paid by the banker on whom it is drawn is evidence of the receipt by the payee of the sum payable by the cheque'. To overcome the problem of those bank customers (such as insurance companies) that still require a receipt, the banks started the practice of requiring that when a form of receipt on the back of the cheque is to be signed the cheque must bear a large 'R' on the front. This serves as a warning to the collecting and paying bankers to check that the receipt has been signed, even though the cheque may have been paid in by the payee to his own account.

6.4 The Collecting Bank

A collecting banker's liability is to the customer for whom he acts as agent when he collects a cheque, bill of exchange or other negotiable instrument, and to the true owner if the banker commits the tort of conversion by collecting the instrument on behalf of a customer who has no title to it.

The Cheques Act 1957, s.4., protects a banker who collects payment of a cheque in good faith and without negligence and stipulates that the banker is not negligent by reason only of failure to be concerned with the absence of (or irregularity in) endorsement of a cheque. The scope of this section of the Act was increased by the Cheques Act 1992 to include the new Account Payee cheques (see p. 95). To get the protection of s.4. the banker must collect the cheque for a customer, i.e. a person for whom an account has been opened by the bank, and for the collection to be done in good faith within the context of s.90. of the Bills of Exchange Act it must be done honestly, whether it is done negligently or not. The banker must act with reasonable care if he is not to be accused of negligence, and in this connection following the 'usual banking practice' is obviously of importance. This fact was clearly established in the case of *Marfani and Co. Ltd v. Midland Bank Ltd* (1968), when in the Court of Appeal Lord Justice Diplock expressed the view that the facts which ought to be known to the banker must depend on current banking practice, and change as that practice changes. He said that cases decided 30 years ago, when the use of banking facilities was less wide-spread, might not be a reliable guide to what the duty of a careful banker is today. The courts should examine current banking practice and decide whether it meets the standard of care required from the prudent banker. Banking facilities have increased even more rapidly since then, of course, and there have been changes in banking practice (note the comments on taking up references on p. 74).

There have been many cases in which collecting banks have been accused of negligence, and we shall not examine them in detail in this book. However, there are some acts of negligence by bankers that have resulted in changes in banking practice:

1   Failure to obtain the name of the customer's employers: *Savory and Co.* v. *Lloyds Bank Ltd* (1932)
2   Failure to obtain references in respect of a new customer unknown to the bank: *Ladbroke and Co* v. *Todd* (1914), and failure to check on the authenticity of a reference: *Guardians of St John's Hampstead* v. *Barclays Bank* (1923) and *Lumsden and Co.* v. *London Trustee Savings Bank* (1971)
3   Collecting a cheque for an official of a company, i.e. paid into his private account: *Underwood* v. *Bank of Liverpool and Martins Bank* (1924) and *Orbit Mining and Trading Co. Ltd* v. *Westminster Bank* (1963)
4   Collecting for an agent's private account cheques payable to him in his private capacity as agent, or cheques drawn by him as attorney: *Bute (Marquess of)* v. *Barclays Bank* (1955) and *Midland Bank Ltd* v. *Reckitt and Others* (1933)
5   Collecting for a company's account cheques payable to another company: *London and Montrose Shipbuilding and Repairing Co.* v. *Barclays Bank* (1926)
6   Collecting cheques inconsistent with the customer's business or private activities: *Nu-Stilo Footwear Ltd* v. *Lloyds Bank* (1956)
7   Collecting third party cheques without appropriate enquiries:
    (i)   where a customer's account has been unsatisfactory: *Motor Traders Guarantee Corporation Ltd* v. *Midland Bank and Others* (1937)
    (ii)   cheques marked 'account payee': *House Property Co. of London Ltd and Others* v. *London County and Westminster Bank* (1915)
    (iii) where circumstances warrant enquiry – cheques payable to a partnership: *Baker* v. *Barclays Bank* (1955)

In the case of *Lumsden and Co.* v. *London Trustee Savings Bank* (1971), the defence of contributory negligence was allowed for the first time to a banker sued for conversion. This decision in favour of the bank might in effect have been reversed by the Torts (Interference with Goods) Act 1977, but s.47 of the Banking Act 1979 restored the situation to what it had been before. S.47 reads: 'In any circumstances in which proof of absence of negligence on the part of a banker would be a defence in proceedings by reason of s.4 of the Cheques Act 1957, a defence of contributory negligence shall also be available to the banker notwithstanding the provisions of S.11(1) of the Torts (Interference with Goods) Act 1977'.

A collecting banker does not need to rely on the provisions of the Cheques Act 1957 for protection if he can demonstrate that he is the holder for value of a cheque presented for payment. To demonstrate this, the banker would have to show that he has given value for the cheque and therefore is collecting it in his own right and not as agent for a customer. If the banker can establish himself as the holder in due course the banker can claim this in defence to an action for conversion.

A holder for value

A banker is deemed to be a holder for value:

1   Where he cashes a third party cheque for a customer or cashes a cheque for a customer of another bank or branch and there is no open credit arrangement
2   If a banker has a lien on a cheque which, for instance, has been returned unpaid and to debit the customer's account would cause it to be overdrawn
3   Where a banker takes a cheque as a specific reduction of an overdraft – this would not apply if a cheque was paid in in the normal course of business for the credit of an overdrawn account
4   Where the customer is allowed to draw against the cheque before it is cleared, provided there is an implied or expressly declared contract for him to do so

A holder in due course

A holder in due course of a cheque (or other bill of exchange) is a holder who has taken the cheque complete and regular on the face of it, under two conditions:

1   That he or she became a holder of it before it was overdue, and without notice that it had been previously dishonoured, if such was the fact
2   That he or she took the cheque in good faith and for value, and that at the time the cheque was negotiated he or she had no notice of any defect in the title of the person who negotiated it

From the wording of this you will appreciate that the concept of a holder in due course is very much related to the concept of negotiability, and therefore is more the concern of the holder of a bill of exchange other than a cheque. This is especially so now that the common form of cheque is the Account Payee type which cannot be transferred. However, if the banker takes a cheque for collection in good faith and without negligence, and can demonstrate that he gave value for it (see holder for value above), he may get the protection of being a holder in due course. Every holder of a bill of exchange (including a cheque) is *prima facie* deemed to be a holder in due course, and it is incumbent upon anyone taking an action in court to prove that the collecting bank is not a holder in due course. The concept of holder in due course has been tested in the courts on many occasions, but it is beyond the scope of this book to look into the ruling of the court in particular cases. A more thorough examination of the law is of course required in preparing for the Associateship examinations of the Chartered Institute of Bankers.

6.5   The Paying Bank

The paying bank must pay a customer's cheque provided it is properly drawn and there are sufficient funds on the account or the customer has made appropriate arrangements for an overdraft facility which covers payment of the cheque. However, the cheque must not be a stale cheque or post-dated, nor must there be any legal barrier to payment.

Stale and post-dated cheques

A 'stale' cheque is one which has been in circulation for a lengthy period of time without being presented for payment. Generally bankers will not pay a cheque after 6 months from its date unless the drawer confirms that it should be paid. Endorsees are completely discharged from liability if there is an unreasonable delay in presentation for payment, but the drawer remains liable on a cheque for 6 years from its date of issue (Limitation Act 1939).

   If a cheque is post-dated, it must not be paid until on or after the due date. The customer's mandate is to pay it on the due date and he would be within his rights to stop payment of the cheque before that date, or the customer may fail or die in the meantime.

Legal barriers to payment

There are six legal barriers to payment:

1   **Customer's death**: immediately a bank receives notice of a customer's death, no further cheques may be paid
2   **Mental incapacity**: if it is known that the customer's mental condition is such that he or she cannot manage his or her own affairs then cheques should not be paid; if there is doubt concerning a customer's condition then it may be necessary for a court order to be obtained by a relative under the Mental Health Act 1983. If an order is issued under the Act there cannot be any further transactions on the customer's account without the court's approval.

3   **Notice of bankruptcy**: immediately (but not until) notice of a bankruptcy petition against the customer is received no further payments must be made from the account.
4   **Receiving or winding-up order**: once a receiving order or winding-up order against a customer **has been made** – not when notice of it has been received – the account must be stopped and cheques returned unpaid.
5   **Garnishee order**: if a creditor has obtained a judgment against the bank's customer, he may obtain a garnishee order and serve it on the bank. The bank must then hold the balance on the account in favour of the creditor – which of course means that any of the customer's cheques received after the order has been served must not be paid.
6   **Court injunction**: if for any other reason a court orders that the account must be frozen then no further payments must be made from the account unless or until the order is lifted.

Defects in presenter's title

Quite apart from these legal barriers, the paying banker must be careful not to pay a cheque if he is aware of a defect in the presenter's title to the cheque or right to be dealing with it – if, for instance, it is apparent that the presenter is mis-applying a company's funds or is an undischarged bankrupt.

If a banker is aware of any defect, then he or she cannot claim to have paid the cheque in due course, i.e. in good faith and in the ordinary course of business without any notice of defect of title (s.60, Bills of Exchange Act 1882) and, if it is a crossed cheque, without negligence (s.80).

Is the cheque properly drawn?

As far as being properly drawn is concerned, there are a number of details that the banker must look out for (see Figure 6.5):

1   If there is a material alteration to the cheque the alteration must be authenti-cated by the drawer's initials or signature near to the alteration. 'Materially altered' means an alteration to the date, the amount in words and/or figures, the payee's name, or any crossing.
2   The cheque must be signed by the drawer.
3   If the cheque has been mutilated it may be wise to seek confirmation that it should be paid, possibly by contacting the drawer or, more likely, sending the cheque back unpaid with a request that the mutilation should be con-firmed. If, for instance the cheque has been torn in half and then repaired there is the possibility that it was meant to be destroyed. Sometimes cheques are inadvertently torn by the collecting bank, in which case the acceptable practice is for the bank to certify on the back that it was torn by them.

102

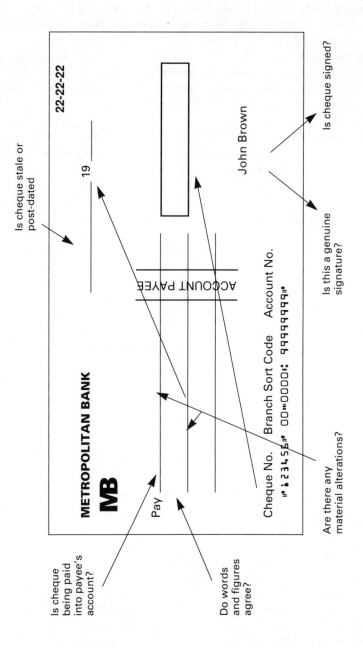

Figure 6.5   What the banker has to look for

4   Where the amounts in words and figures differ, it is the usual practice these
days to pay the amount in words. However, the practice is somewhat flexible
and a bank may decide to pay the lower amount if it thinks the customer's
mandate is unclear, or to send the cheque back unpaid with the answer
'words and figures differ'. Obviously a deciding factor here is likely to be
the amount involved – a bank is hardly likely to concern itself very much
about a difference in the pence. The collecting bank is often helpful by indicating on the cheque the amount claimed by the payee and it is that amount
that will be claimed through the clearing.

5   If the drawer's signature does not match up with the specimen signature held
by the paying bank, the bank would be quite in order to send the cheque back
unpaid with the answer; 'drawer's signature requires confirmation'. However, if the bank is seriously suspicious that the signature has been forged,
then it has a legal obligation to notify the customer without delay – it is one
of the duties of the banker.

6   If a cheque is undated a bank could return the cheque because of the
omission, as its mandate is unclear. However, the definition of a cheque in
the Bills of Exchange Act (see p. 90) does not state that a cheque must be
dated, and s.3(4) says that a bill of exchange is not invalid if it is undated.

Stopped cheques

A customer of a bank is entitled to stop payment of a cheque that he has drawn
provided that the bank on which it is drawn is notified before the cheque is presented for payment and that the cheque was not supported by a cheque guarantee
card at the time it was drawn. The notice that payment is countermanded must be
in writing, but the banks will accept verbal instructions provided that they are
later confirmed in writing. A problem could arise of course if that written confirmation was not received before the cheque was presented for payment. The
usual procedure under such circumstances is to return the cheque unpaid with the
answer 'payment countermanded – confirmation awaited'.

Risks of non-payment

If there are no reasons why a particular cheque should not be paid the banker will
return it unpaid at his peril. He would be in breach of contract and might be sued
for damages for libel. It is usual to mark a cheque 'Refer to Drawer' if it is sent
back because of insufficient funds rather than to mark it 'Insufficient Funds' as
the latter statement is obviously likely to be considered libellous, whereas the
former can only be said to infer that there are insufficient funds because of the
common usage of the phrase in such circumstances. If a customer who is a businessman can show that his business has suffered because of the slur on his

reputation caused by the wrongful return of a cheque, he might be able to claim very substantial damages.

Protection for the paying banker

Another risk to the paying banker is that he might pay a cheque to a person other than the rightful owner and be sued for conversion. However, the banker is protected by s.80 of the Bills of Exchange Act if the cheque he pays is a crossed cheque and it is paid in accordance with the crossing, in good faith and without negligence. Under such circumstances the banker is then in the same legal position as he would have been had he paid the money to the rightful owner. This section of the Act was extended by the Cheques Act 1992 to include cheques made not transferable by the Account Payee crossing.

If s.80 cannot be said to apply (because the cheque is not crossed, for instance), the banker is protected by s.1 of the Cheques Act 1957 which states that the bank is under no obligation to show that an endorsement was valid, and that the bank is deemed to have discharged the cheque by payment to the holder even if there is a defect in the endorsement, provided that the bank acted in good faith and in the ordinary course of business.

Review Questions

1　How are bills of exchange used in modern times as a means of settlement in international trade? (6.2)
2　Can bills of exchange be used by exporters as a means of obtaining finance? (6.2)
3　What are the advantages of using a bill of exchange? (6.2)
4　Give the official definition of a bill of exchange and from this the definition of a cheque. (6.2, 6.3)
5　Can a cheque be conditional? (6.3)
6　What is meant by the term 'in writing' with reference to a cheque? (6.3)
7　Why have cheques become so popular as a method of payment? (6.3)
8　How would you distinguish between the drawer and the drawee of a cheque? (6.3)
9　Who is the payee of a cheque? (6.3)
10　If the payee of a cheque endorses it over to another person, is he the endorser or the endorsee? (6.3)
11　How would you distinguish between a special endorsement and an endorsement in blank? (6.3)
12　What is the purpose of crossing a cheque? (6.3)

Review Questions   cont'd.

13   How would you distinguish between a general crossing and a special crossing? (6.3)

14   Who may cross a cheque? (6.3)

15   What is the significance of the 'Account Payee' crossing on a cheque? (6.3)

16   What is the significance of a 'Not transferable' crossing on a cheque? (6.3)

17   What is involved in the concept of negotiability? (6.3)

18   What was the main purpose of the Cheques Act 1957? How did the banks later limit the effectiveness of the Act? (6.3)

19   Is it necessary to ask for a receipt when making a payment by cheque? (6.3)

20   What is the collecting bank's responsibility to the customer for whom it collects a cheque? (6.4)

21   To what extent is the collecting banker responsible to the owner of a cheque (cite the Cheques Acts in this connection)? (6.4)

22   What is meant by the term 'Usual banking practice'? Does this change with changing circumstances? (6.4)

23   What are the various circumstances in which collecting banks have been found guilty of negligence? (6.4)

24   What is a holder for value? (6.4)

25   What is a holder in due course? (6.4)

26   What is meant by a stale cheque? (6.5)

27   Can a post-dated cheque be paid? (6.5)

28   What are the six legal barriers to payment of a cheque? (6.5)

29   What is meant by a 'material alteration' to a cheque? (6.5)

30   Can a mutilated cheque be paid? (6.5)

31   If the amounts in words and figures on a cheque differ, what action should a bank take? (6.5)

32   If the drawer's signature on a cheque does not match up with the specimen signature held by the bank, what action should the bank take? (6.5)

33   Can an undated cheque be paid? (6.5)

34   What is meant by stopping a cheque? (6.5)

35   If there is no technical or legal reason for non-payment and there are sufficient funds and the paying banker returns the cheque unpaid marked 'Insufficient funds', what are the banker's liabilities to the customer? (6.5)

36   If a paying banker pays a cheque to the wrong person, what action might the true owner take? (6.5)

37   What protection is provided for the paying banker by the Bills of Exchange Act and the Cheques Acts? (6.5)

Past Examination Questions

1   (a) Your customer Mr. Paul Gazzer wants to pay the following cheque
         into your branch for credit to his wife's account. Her name is Sally.

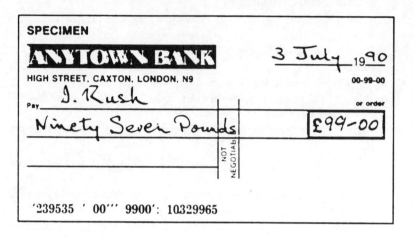

Reverse of cheque

Would you accept the cheque for credit to her account? Explain the
reasons for arriving at your decision.

(10 marks)

Past Examination Questions   cont'd.

(b) The following cheque arrives through the clearing for payment.
Your customer Mr B. Roake has a balance of £210.57, but his
salary will be paid into the account in 2 days time.

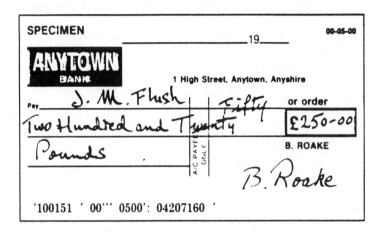

SIGNATURE CARD

Would you pay the cheque? Explain the reasons for arriving at
your decision.

(10 marks)

2   (a) Give the definition of a cheque.

(6 marks)

(b) Draw a rough sketch of the cheque described in each of the
following situations, filling in the appropriate details (including
crossings); then give the explanations required.

Past Examination Questions   cont'd.

(i)   You want to pay a cheque to Jim Smith for £320.00 and you want to ensure security for yourself. Draw the cheque and explain the banking significance of the details you have included. You know that Jim wants to pass the cheque to A. Fella. Is this possible? If so, explain how it can be done.

(10 marks)

(ii)   You are posting a cheque to Eva Stick for £45.00 for goods received. You are worried that, should the cheque be lost, someone might try to pay it into his account. Explain how this could be done, and show on the cheque how you could prevent this from happening.

(4 marks)

3   (a)   Define the role of:
   (i)   the collecting banker

   (ii)   the paying banker.

(6 marks)

   (b)   (i)   The following cheque is handed in over the counter by your customer Ray Bok. List the factors that you would consider when deciding whether to collect the cheque for him.

(6 marks)

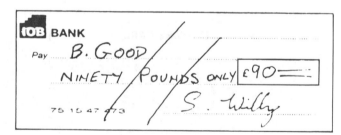

Past Examination Questions   cont'd.

(ii) The paying bank receives the following cheque through the clearing system signed by its customer Benny Ton. He has £92 in his account and you know that he regularly overdraws his account by a small amount just before payday. His salary is due in next week. What factors would you consider when deciding what to do with the cheque?

(8 marks)

IOB BANK   1ST OCT 1992

Pay MARK SPENCER

ONE HUNDRED THOUSAND POUNDS ONLY   £1000 —

75.15 47 473   NOT NEGOTIABLE   Benny Ton

Reverse of cheque

Mark Spencer.

7 Other methods of payment

┌─ **Chapter objectives** ───

When you have carefully studied this chapter you should be able to:
- Give an account of the bank giro system
- Explain the systems of direct debits and standing orders and compare one with the other
- Give an account of the debit and credit clearing systems, including the town clearing
- Distinguish between the CHAPS and BACS methods of settlement
- Explain the purpose of Switch and Delta cards
- Define a bankers' draft and explain why it might be used
└──

7.1 Introduction

In Chapter 6 we concentrated on cheques, which have been the main method of payment up to the present time. Now we need to look at the clearing systems and in detail at the alternative methods of payment which have come into their own during the second half of the twentieth century and which may eventually overtake the cheque system in terms of volume and value. The cheque system is very costly to operate even with up-to-date electronic methods of sorting and recording, and the banks have welcomed the introduction of electronic methods of actually transmitting funds from customer to customer and from bank to bank, which are much cheaper and quicker to operate.

7.2 The Bank Giro System

Credit transfers

As an alternative to drawing a cheque a person who has a debt to settle can do so by using the bank giro system, provided he knows the bank and branch and the account number of the creditor and that the creditor is in agreement with this method of payment.

The person initiating the payment writes out a credit transfer form (a bank giro form) indicating the name of the account holder to be credited, the bank and branch at which the account is kept, and the account number. The amount to be transferred is normally paid in cash to the bank which is to send the transfer, but if the person initiating the transfer is a customer at the bank he may draw a cheque which will be debited to his account. The credit transfer is then sent up to the bank's clearing department and taken to the Clearing House where batches of credit transfers are handed over to the banks whose customers' accounts are to be credited. We shall be looking at this credit clearing process in more detail in Section 7.4 below.

The bank giro system saves the debtor the effort and expense of writing and posting a cheque to the beneficiary, and the beneficiary is saved the trouble of having to visit a bank to pay in the cheque. However, the debtor has to visit a bank to initiate the transfer, but if when he does so a number of credit transfers are sent off (maybe all bills are saved up until the end of the month), the journey may seem more worthwhile. The beneficiaries receive notification of giro payments into their accounts by means of their statements of account. Many beneficiaries encourage the use of this method of payment by issuing the debtor with a book of bank giro credits with the details already written in, often in magnetic ink which can be picked up electronically by the banks handling the transfers, and thus saving the debtor time and inconvenience. Local authorities do this as an alternative to receiving payment in cash at the town hall counters in respect of the council tax or council house rents and similar payments. In the same way public utilities such as the gas, electricity and water boards issue credit transfers for the payment of bills and the building societies will do likewise, if requested to do so, for monthly mortgage repayments.

The bank giro must be distinguished from the Girobank which is operated through the post offices by the Alliance and Leicester Building Society (see p. 26).

7.3   Direct Debits and Standing Orders

Direct debits

As an alternative to issuing their customers with supplies of bank giro forms, the local authorities, public utilities and other institutions which receive very large numbers of regular payments might well prefer to have direct debit mandates from their customers which permit them to initiate claims upon their bank accounts (see Figure 7.1). They can then be more certain that the payments are made when due and may even be able to vary the amount as necessary. The direct debit mandate is issued both to the beneficiary and to the bank; it authorises the beneficiary to make claims upon the customer's account at a specified bank and branch and authorises the bank to make the payments. The mandate may specify the amount(s) to be paid but can be open-ended and simply authorise the bank to

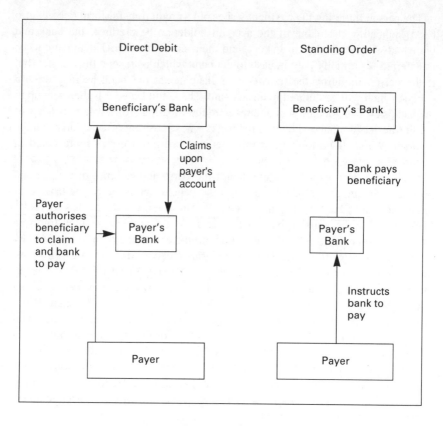

Figure 7.1   Direct debits and standing orders

pay whatever claims the beneficiary may make upon his account. This latter arrangement is convenient for such things as annual subscriptions which tend to go up with inflation from year to year. It saves the institution the bother of having to get a new mandate signed by the member each time the amount changes. Where very large numbers of regular monthly payments are involved (e.g. mortgage payments, insurance premiums, rents, etc.), the beneficiary may submit the claims to its bank on computer tape or disk to enable the claims to be speedily dealt with through BACS (see below).

Standing orders

Rather than have his account debited with regular payments upon the initiative of the beneficiary, a bank customer may prefer to initiate the payments himself by giving a standing order to the bank. This authorises his bank to make the payments as they fall due and usually states the number of payments to be made or the expiry date of the mandate, though it can simply say 'until further notice'.

Once the standing order has been handed to the bank the customer can forget about when payments are due, they are made automatically for him, but he must make sure that there are sufficient funds on his account to meet the payments because the bank is not obliged to make a payment which overdraws the account without any prior arrangement. Furthermore, if there are insufficient funds for a payment to be made on the due date, the bank does not have to make that payment should funds be paid in a few days later (see p. 61), but it is the usual practice to notify the customer that the payment was not made.

The essential difference between a direct debit and a standing order is that payments under direct debits are initiated by the creditor, whereas payments by standing order are at the initiative of the debtor. The large institutions prefer direct debits because they can more readily ensure that the payments are received – their claims are paid unless they bounce back unpaid, in which case the process of chasing their customer for payment is triggered off. With standing orders the beneficiary company has the task of checking through its bank statements to ensure that all payments are received and then pursuing those customers who have defaulted. Another point about standing orders is that the debtor's bank has the task of dealing with each standing order separately, and unless several customers are making similar payments, cannot deal with them in bulk. With direct debits, on the other hand, the creditor is usually making a large number of claims and may be prepared to present them to the bank in bulk on tape or disk.

7.4 The debit and credit clearing systems

Debit clearing

We are concerned here primarily with the clearance of cheques though there are other debit items such as bankers' drafts and bankers' payments which are included in the debit clearing (see Figure 7.2).

When a cheque drawn on another bank is paid into the payee's account, receipt of it by the bank is given by a rubber stamp and the cashier's initial on the counterfoil of the paying-in book. At the end of the day, the bank will dispatch that cheque to its clearing department together with all other cheques paid in by customers that are drawn on other banks or other branches. Any cheques paid in that are drawn by other customers of the branch do not need to be cleared, of course, and remain on the premises if they are paid (or are returned unpaid through the post to the customers who paid them in if they are dishonoured). In the specimen cheque in Figure 6.3, one set of magnetic characters along the bottom of the cheque is missing. This is the amount of the cheque, a fact which is not known when the cheque book is prepared for the drawer's use. Before the cheques are sent off to the bank's clearing department this amount is encoded on the cheque so that it can be read by a computer at a later stage.

On Day 2, the clearing department of the bank receives all the bundles of cheques sent to it by the branches the day before and they are checked against the

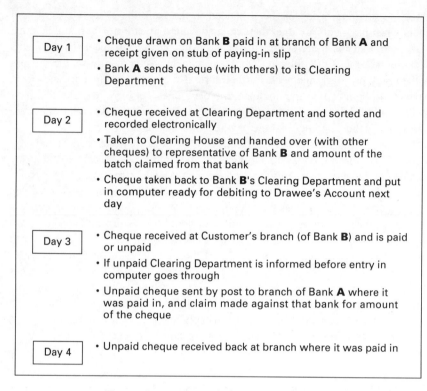

Figure 7.2   The cheque clearing process

tally slips that are sent with them. The cheques are sorted into bank and branch by an electronic reader/sorter machine and batches prepared of cheques to be presented to other banks at the Bankers' Clearing House in London. Cheques on other branches are sent to those branches concerned by the clearing department as there is no need for them to go to the Clearing House. At the Clearing House, each bank hands over to the other banks bundles of cheques drawn by customers of those banks and receives bundles of cheques from the other banks.

The clearing department posts the cheques it receives to the debit of its customers' accounts (including those received from branches that are drawn on other branches); this is done by electronic reader which feeds the account number, cheque number and amount into the computer. These items are not actually debited to the accounts until the next day, by which time the branches on which the cheques are drawn will have been able to notify the clearing department if any of the cheques are not to be paid. The computer produces lists of all the items debited to customers' accounts, and these lists accompany the bundles of cheques that are sent off to the branches at the end of Day 2 of the process.

On Day 3, the bundles of cheques received from the clearing department are listed at the branch and the total checked against the computer list. The process of payment then begins. Each cheque has to be inspected to ensure that there is nothing technically wrong with it – do the words and figures differ? is the cheque stale or mutilated? has the cheque been signed by the drawer? The clerk who is paying the cheques will also have to make sure that payment has not been countermanded. Provided that the drawer has an adequate balance on the account, or that the overdraft limit has not been exceeded, the cheque will be paid. If the manager decides to return a cheque unpaid – whether it be for a legal or technical reason, or because it has been stopped, or because there are insufficient funds on the account – the reason must be written on the cheque. The words 'Cheque out of Date', 'Payment Countermanded', 'Words and Figures Differ', 'Drawer's Signature Required', or 'Drawer Deceased' cause no difficulties for the paying banker in that the customer (the drawer) can hardly object. However, if there are insufficient funds this must not be stated and, instead, the words 'Refer to Drawer' or 'Refer to Drawer – Please Represent' will be used. An unpaid cheque is returned through the post direct to the branch of the bank which presented it for payment, as shown by the rubber stamp across the face of the cheque.

Assuming there are no delays in the post, an unpaid cheque will arrive back at the collecting bank's branch office on Day 4 and that branch will send it by post to the customer who paid it in. It will therefore be Day 5 before the customer who paid the cheque in is aware that the cheque is unpaid, although he may possibly be informed on Day 4 by telephone. (This process could take longer if the collecting bank is not a member of APACS and has to clear cheques through the agency of another bank. Such is the case with the vast majority of overseas banks in London.) The account will be debited with the unpaid cheque on Day 4 and it is for this reason that the large clearing banks expect their customers to allow 4 clear working days before drawing against cheques that have been paid in for collection, and reserve the right to send cheques back unpaid marked 'Effects Not Cleared' if they are drawn prematurely.

To expedite clearance of a cheque a customer may ask for it to be specially cleared, for which he will be charged a set fee. A special presentation involves sending the cheque direct to the bank on which it is drawn through the post, or by hand if it is local. If it is sent by post, the collecting bank telephones the paying bank next day to ascertain whether the cheque is paid or not. If it is paid the paying bank remits the amount of it to the collecting bank through the credit clearing.

Within the City of London a special Town Clearing operates (as distinct from the General Clearing which we have been looking at so far). Banks within walking distance of the Clearing House bundle up cheques of £500,000 or more drawn on other Town branches and send them to the Clearing House by messenger. These are handed over to representatives of the banks concerned and delivered by them to the branches on which they are drawn. Cheques can be presented at the Clearing House up to 3.50 p.m. and any unpaid cheques must be returned by 4.45 p.m. The Town Clearing is restricted to branches of banks within the City of London – they have the letter 'T' against the sorting code in the top right hand corner of the cheque.

The Town Clearing has in the past greatly facilitated the activities within the London money market, and those of the large companies in the City, but to a considerable extent the work of the Town Clearing has been taken over by CHAPS (see below) through which large sums of money are transferred by telegraphic means.

Settlement between the banks for cheques, and for the credit clearing and other forms of clearing mentioned below, is made by offsetting money owed by a bank to other banks against money owed to it. The net amount is settled through the accounts held by the banks at the Bank of England. Settlement for the General Clearing takes place the day after the cheques have actually been exchanged because the cheques are not paid (or returned unpaid) until that day.

Credit clearing

As we saw on p. 111, credit transfers paid in at a bank for the credit of a customer of another bank or branch are sent by the bank receiving the credit to its clearing department (see Figure 7.3). The discerning reader will appreciate that credit giros move through the clearing system in the opposite direction to cheques – whereas a cheque is a **claim for money**, and passes via the clearing from the beneficiary's bank to the debtor's bank, a credit transfer represents a **payment of money** and passes, again through the clearing, but from the debtor's bank to the beneficiary's bank. The cheque clearing is the debit clearing and the bank giro system the credit clearing.

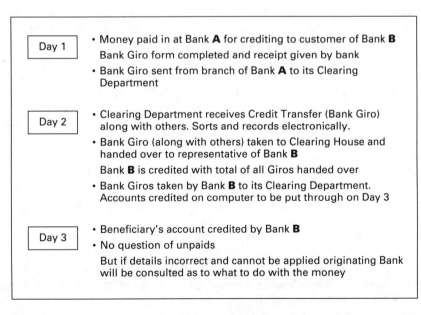

Figure 7.3   The credit clearing process

On the day that the clearing department receives a credit transfer it is taken to the Clearing House where batches of credit transfers are handed over to the banks whose accounts are to be credited. Most credit transfers have the details printed on them in magnetic ink and therefore they can be sorted electronically in the same way as cheques. A giro credit paid in on Day 1 reaches the Clearing House on Day 2, and is handed over to the recipient bank, which then sends it to the appropriate branch to arrive on Day 3. Unlike cheques there is no question of unpaids, but there is the possibility that a credit cannot be identified because the details of the account have been given incorrectly, or the beneficiary's account may have been closed. In such circumstances it would be necessary for the bank receiving the transfer to communicate with the bank that initiated it for instructions as to what to do with the amount received.

Association for Payment Clearing Services (APACS)

In the sections on the debit and credit clearings reference has been made on a number of occasions to the Bankers' Clearing House in London. Up to the mid-1980s this was owned and run by the London clearing banks, but now it comes under the overall control of APACS (Association for Payment Clearing Services) to which the main English, Scottish and Irish banks belong as well as two overseas banks and a number of building societies. APACS has oversight over three limited companies which between them are responsible for the majority of paper clearings and a large part of the electronic money transfers. These are:

1   Cheque and Credit Clearing Co Ltd
2   CHAPS and Town Clearing Co Ltd
3   BACS Ltd

From their names it is obvious that the Cheque and Credit Clearing Co. is responsible for the debit and credit clearings and that CHAPS and Town Clearing Co. is concerned with the Town Clearing, all of which we have looked at. But we have yet to look in detail at CHAPS although we have discussed how it has largely taken over the work of the Town Clearing. We shall also look in detail at the work of BACS Ltd, which is concerned with bulk electronic credit and debit clearings. This brings us on to the subject of electronic funds transfers.

7.5   Electronic Funds Transfers

CHAPS (Clearing House Automated Payment System)

This system facilitates same day credit transfers by electronic means between the banks that are members of the system. The minimum amount for a CHAPS transfer was £5,000 until January 1992, when the limit was removed and consequently transfers may now be made for any amount. Bank customers may give their banks instructions in writing or on the telephone or telex to make CHAPS transfers and larger company customers have computer lines or terminals for the purpose of giving such instructions. There is also a link between CHAPS and SWIFT (Society for Worldwide Interbank Financial Telecommunication), an organisation subscribed to by banks all over the world to facilitate transfers of funds by computer links between them via a central SWIFT computer.

BACS Ltd

This was previously called Bankers' Automated Services Ltd but now simply BACS Ltd. It is concerned with handling the multitude of debit and credit transfers that are generated by direct debits and standing orders as well as payments of wages and salaries, pensions and a whole host of other payments that corporate bank customers give their banks instructions to make by electronic means. The majority of the transactions are prepared on tapes or disks by the customers themselves so that they can be fed into the BACS computer in North London. The process takes 3 working days, as follows:

Day 1   The data is received by BACS and is processed and sent to members. In some cases the data is received several days before it is to be processed by BACS.

Day 2   The members receive the data from BACS and prepare the necessary debit and credit entries to go on to their customers' accounts, but they are not activated until the next day.

Day 3   The transactions are debited and credited to the customers' accounts as cleared funds, and the necessary transfers made in the accounts of the banks at the Bank of England to settle the differences due in respect of the totals of the debit and credit transactions.

EFTPOS (Electronic Funds Transfer Point of Sale)

For many years the banks in the UK have endeavoured to establish a system in conjunction with retailers and British Telecom which would enable retailers to make an electronic transfer from the customer's bank account to its own. A fourth member company of APACS was set up for the purpose (EFTPOS UK Ltd). The joint plans did not come to fruition, however, and the company simple functions as an advisory body to APACS. Instead the banks have adapted their existing plastic service cards (one card which serves as an ATM card and also a cheque guarantee card) to serve also as a Switch or Delta card, or have issued new cards for the purpose. These cards can be used at those retailers who have the appropriate terminals by their tills for the cards to be 'swiped' and the amount of the transaction electronically transmitted as a claim upon the bank account of the customer. The customer signs an authority for the debit to take place and the slip for this purpose is produced automatically by the till. The process is intended to speed up payment at the point of sale in order to avoid queues and also to reduce the handling of cash and the delays that are caused by the customer manually writing out a cheque which has to be verified against the customer's cheque guarantee card. The use of plastic cards is dealt with in detail in Chapter 10.

7.6   Bankers' Drafts

A bankers' draft is in effect a cheque drawn by a bank upon itself (or possibly upon another bank) to provide a customer with a means of payment which is more readily acceptable than his own cheque because of the fact that it is drawn by a bank. A customer's own cheque would be very acceptable if it were accompanied by a cheque guarantee card, but the amount of such a guarantee will be limited to £50 (or possibly £100 or £250). For payments above that amount the purchaser of a car, for instance, is not likely to find that the car salesman will be willing to part with the car until the cheque is cleared. The banker's draft overcomes this problem. The customer asks his bank to write a draft for the sum required and his account is debited with that sum plus commission. He then pays for the car or other large item with the draft.

Up to fairly recently solicitors always used banker's drafts when completing for the purchase of a house on behalf of a client. Instead they now transfer funds by electronic means through CHAPS, provided that they have access to a gateway into CHAPS, i.e. a settlement bank. The large high street banks all offer this facility, but for smaller banks, such as the foreign banks in London, it may be necessary for them to pass on their solicitor customer's request for a CHAPS transfer to another bank which is a settlement bank.

Figure 7.4 summarises the ways that deposits can be transferred.

Review Examination Questions

1   What is the bank giro system? (7.2)
2   What are the advantages to (a) the debtor and (b) the creditor of the credit transfer system? (7.2)
3   Who are the main users of credit transfers? (7.2)
4   How does a direct debit work? (7.3)
5   Who initiates a standing order? (7.3)
6   What are the points of difference between a direct debit and a standing order? (7.3)
7   By what steps does a cheque move through the clearing process? (7.4)
8   Which set of magnetic characters is missing from a book of cheques? (7.4)

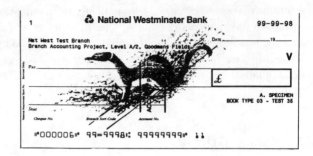

PLUS:
BACS ELECTRONIC PAYMENTS
STANDING ORDERS
DIRECT DEBITS
BANKERS' DRAFTS

Figure 7.4   Ways of transferring deposits

┌─ **Review Examination Questions cont'd** ─────────────────┐

9   When a cheque is received through the clearing, what does the recipient bank do with it? (7.4)

10 How is a cheque specially cleared? (7.4)

11 How does the Town Clearing operate? (7.4)

12 How do the banks settle with one another for the transactions that pass through the clearing house? (7.4)

13 How would you distinguish between the debit clearing and the credit clearing? How long does the credit clearing process take? (7.4)

14 What are the functions of APACS? (7.4)

15 How does CHAPS work? How long does it take to transfer funds? (7.5)

16 Why was BACS set up? Explain how it operates. (7.5)

17 What is meant by EFTPOS? Is the system actually in operation? (7.5)

18 How may a bankers' draft be used to make a payment? (7.6)

└──┘

┌─ **Past Examination Questions** ──────────────────────────┐

1   Bank customers often need to pay money into the bank accounts of organisations or individuals, e.g. paying bills, making salary payments. Give **one** example of how these payments can be made and how the system operates using:

(a) a paper system   (*10 marks*)

(b) an electronic system.   (*10 marks*)

2   Banks use a variety of clearing systems to debit and credit their customers' accounts.
Briefly describe the system used in each of the following situations, and give one benefit customers obtain from the system:

(a) A company wants to pay its workforce through their bank accounts.   (*10 marks*)

(b) A customer within the City of London wants to clear a cheque for £500,000* as quickly as possible.   (*6 marks*)

(c) A solicitor wants £90,000 remitted to another firm of solicitors on the same day. Both firms bank with 'gateway' or settlement banks.
                                                          (*4 marks*)

*Question amended to increase amount from £20,000 in original.

└──┘

Bank deposits and lending

Chapter objectives

When you have carefully studied this chapter you should be able to:
- Examine the range of accounts the retail banks provide for personal customers, including the various savings and investment accounts
- Comment on the various types of advances and indicate the purposes for which each type is appropriate
- Explain the principles of bank lending
- Explain the reasons for saving

8.1 Introduction

In Chapter 7 we examined the methods of payment, one of the three main services which the retail banks provide (referred to in Chapter 2). In this chapter we shall examine in detail the other two services, bank deposits and bank lending. We shall place particular emphasis on the services rendered to personal customers as this is what is required in the Business of Banking syllabus.

8.2 The Acceptance of Deposits

Current accounts

Whereas up to the 1970s the retail banks offered personal customers only three types of account – current account, deposit account and savings account – they now offer a wide range of accounts in order to attract customers in competition with one another and with the building societies and other financial intermediaries. It is essential for the banking student to be familiar with the types and purposes of these accounts, but as each bank has its own range of accounts with various names and terms and conditions it is impossible for him to be familiar with them all; instead, they can be put into categories. We shall endeavour to do that here, but if you have access to a list of the products offered by a particular bank then you would be wise to study it and to categorise them into the types commented upon below.

All current accounts are designed to attract deposits by offering the facility of being able to withdraw funds by cheque and, under certain conditions, the facility of being able to overdraw if need be. They are designed to meet the needs of the depositor with an income (or maybe several incomes from different sources, e.g. salary or pension, dividends, rents, annuity), from which day-to-day living expenditure is to be financed. This has always been the nature of a current account, but in recent years the banks have made them more attractive by offering additional facilities such as interest on the cleared balance from day-to-day, a bank service card which may be used to withdraw cash through an ATM, as a cheque guarantee card and, possibly for transferring funds by Switch or Delta. Furthermore, some current accounts provide for an automatic overdraft facility up to a prescribed limit, which could possibly specify that interest will not be charged for borrowing up to a specified sum and beyond that a rate of interest and a fixed quarterly commission charge which is generally more favourable than that charged to customers who borrow without such an account. As far as commission charges generally are concerned, up to the time of writing banks do not charge commission on current accounts provided they are kept in credit, but this may well change and the student reader should keep abreast of developments in this connection.

As we have seen, the current account provides the three main facilities which any current account must offer, i.e. the acceptance of deposits, the provision of credit (loans and overdrafts), and a means of transferring funds from the account to third parties. At one time these transfers were done by drawing cheques or arranging standing orders, but more recently, direct debits were introduced as well as electronic methods of transfer, e.g. the debit card such as the Switch or Delta card, or a gold card.

High interest cheque accounts

For customers who wish to keep a larger than usual sum of money available for immediate use at any time, but who look for a good rate of interest on the outstanding balance, the banks offer high interest current accounts. They tend to specify a minimum balance that must be maintained on the account or, alternatively, set tiered or banded rates of interest to encourage the customer to leave a large balance on the account. A tiered interest rate structure provides for the high rate to apply to the whole balance; for instance, if the bank pays 5 per cent interest on balances up to £2,000 and 7 per cent on balances beyond that sum, immediately the balance reaches £2001 the higher rate of 7 per cent applies to the whole sum. With banded rates this is not so and, using the same example, a balance of £5,000 would attract 5 per cent on the first £2,000 and 7 per cent on the remaining £3,000.

Some banks lay down a minimum size of cheque for their high interest cheque accounts to discourage heavy use for small transactions, preferring the customer to use the high interest account as a topping up account for his ordinary current account. Some banks encourage this by offering to automatically transfer sums from the high interest account to the current account when the balance on the latter falls below a set amount.

Gold accounts

For those customers with incomes above a certain sum (maybe £20,000 per annum) some of the banks offer a gold card facility. The gold card is a debit card which is linked to the MasterCard or Visa International System, and can be used for purchases for an unlimited amount at home or abroad. The customer receives a statement once a month which has to be settled by cheque or by automatic debit to the customer's gold current account by a direct debit arrangement. Whilst the card is a debit card rather than a credit card, there is usually, however, a generous unsecured overdraft limit on which a special low rate of interest is charged. In the case of the NatWest Gold Plus Service the limit is £10,000 and the rate of interest 3 1/2 per cent above base rate. In this account the overdraft may be converted to a loan, by arrangement, at the same favourable rate. No normal bank charges (as distinct from interest) are levied by NatWest on their Gold Account even if it is overdrawn, but there is a set annual fee. The NatWest account also provides for free travel insurance for the gold card holder, free protection for keys and credit cards and a number of other attractive features, which are especially appropriate for the high income-earner who travels a great deal in connection with his work.

Savings accounts

As always, savings accounts are designed to provide a home for savings on which interest is received, but usually cheques cannot be drawn on them. However, some banks now supply ATM cards to savings account holders in order to meet the competition from some of the building societies. One bank, Lloyds Bank, even permits standing orders and direct debits on savings accounts.

Some banks offer a special type of savings account for customers who are prepared to pay in a regular monthly sum and on which only a limited number of withdrawals per year are permitted. They are rewarded by higher rates of interest than on ordinary savings accounts.

Most of the banks offer special savings accounts for those under 18 years of age on which good rates of interest are paid in order to attract the young people to the bank as potential current account holders.

Investment accounts

For customers with funds to invest that are not likely to be required for immediate withdrawal, comparatively high rates of interest are offered by the banks on
a wide range of investment accounts, most of them similar to those offered by the
building societies. The larger the sum invested and the longer the period of notice
the account holder is willing to give, the higher the rate of interest. Even though a
deposit is subject, for instance, to 6 months' notice for withdrawal, repayment of
the deposit can usual be obtained immediately but subject to loss of interest on
the amount withdrawn for a set number of days or months.

Money market deposits

For large investors the banks will place money on the money market for their
customers on terms ranging from overnight to 12 months. Usually they are fixed-
term deposits but some are repaid without notice, if required. The rates of interest
paid are those available on the money market at the time and they vary with the
length of time of the deposit. Deposits are normally for £10,000 or more.

Certificates of deposit

For customers who are willing to deposit large sums (£50,000 or more), for a
number of years (maybe 5 years), the banks offer certificates of deposit (CDs) on
which very favourable rates of interest are paid. The certificate acknowledges
receipt of the deposit and specifies the rate of interest that is to be paid on it, and
when the sum is repayable. Usually an amount in sterling is involved, but CDs
are issued in US dollars as well. CDs are negotiable and therefore the holder may
obtain his money back (or some of it) by selling the CD on the open market. The
amount that he receives will depend upon the attractiveness of the CD as an
investment at the time it is sold. If the rate of interest received on the CD is
higher than the current level of interest at the time then it is possible that the
holder will receive more for it than its nominal value, though the opposite may of
course apply.

TESSA accounts

These are tax exempt special savings accounts which, as the name suggests, offer
tax-free rates of interest. This special scheme was established by the government
to operate from January 1991, to encourage savings. Each individual is allowed
only one TESSA account and therefore they have to be registered to ensure that
the system is not abused. The maximum sum that can be invested over a 5-year
period is £9,000 and, of this, only £3,000 is permitted in Year 1, £1,800 per year

in Years 2, 3 and 4 and £600 in Year 5. If the sums invested are held for the full 5-year period no income tax is deducted and TESSAs do not have to be declared for tax purposes, but if any of the interest is withdrawn before the end of that period, tax has to be deducted from it, and any withdrawal of capital leads to loss of all tax exemption. The rates of interest paid by the banks and the buildings societies on TESSA accounts are at the discretion of the institution concerned in the same way as interest on other accounts. Account holders are permitted to switch from one bank or building society to another but may, in some cases, have to pay a penalty to the institution losing the account – this depends upon the terms laid down in the particular scheme.

The reasons for saving

Before leaving the subject of the acceptance of deposits it would be as well if we looked at the reasons why people save because, obviously, these reasons will determine the type of bank account the depositor will look for and whether in fact he may go to a competitor to purchase some other financial product which better suits his purpose, if the bank does not itself sell that product.

The reasons for saving can be summarised as follows:

1   Fairly immediate needs: such as household and personal expenditure during the weeks or months ahead. A current or budget account would be appropriate for these.
2   Emergencies: the unexpected breakdown of a domestic appliance or a plumbing bill or car repair. For these a residual balance on a current account might be appropriate; whilst for such things as extended sickness or unemployment a savings account of some kind might be appropriate.
3   Safety: it is wiser to deposit surplus cash with a bank even if no interest is paid on it, than to carry it around or leave it in the house. A current account would be appropriate.
4   For a particular purpose: such as buying a car, a house or a holiday. Some form of savings account on which interest is paid would be appropriate.
5   Future security: for retirement and/or to hedge against inflation which over the years will erode spending power. Some form of longer-term investment is called for which will build up a capital fund and maybe a regular income when it is most needed.

In deciding what type of a bank account or financial product is appropriate for a particular purpose, the customer must bear in mind three factors and decide which of them is the most important in his particular circumstances:

● Degree of risk
● Availability
● Rate of return

If he is looking for a high return on his money then he may be prepared to take a higher degree of risk by, for instance, investing in shares the value of which could go down as well as up. Furthermore when the value of shares goes down the holder has less accessibility to his money because the amount he would receive would be lower, possibly even lower than the amount he put into them in the first place. Alternatively, he might get his high return by investing his funds on a long-term deposit account, e.g. subject to 6 months' notice, which may be quite safe but he will have difficulty in getting access to his funds in an emergency.

If he wants the funds to be available to him at any time then he will want to deposit them on immediate or short-term notice. For this the rate of return will be lower than that paid on deposits or investments which are subject to a longer period of notice for repayment.

8.3 Bank Lending

Overdrafts

Just as there are now many different types of accounts available to the customer so there are many different types of borrowing facilities, or lending products as they tend to be called. We need to examine them in detail. For some of these security has to be lodged, but for others this is not necessary – we shall examine this aspect of bank lending in Section 8.4 below.

As we saw in Section 8.2, some types of current account provide for an automatic overdraft up to a certain limit and at a set rate of interest. In some instances these are free of interest (for students, for example) but these are special cases and are not all that common.

An overdraft facility permits the account holder to draw cheques in excess of his balance (sometimes even today referred to as 'going into the red' because when bank accounting was done manually overdrawn balances were shown in the ledgers in red ink; today they are shown with DR against them, i.e. debit balance, as distinct from those marked CR or C, i.e. credit balance).

For the majority of overdrafts, arrangements are made with the bank in advance and the purpose of the borrowing is stated and the length of the borrowing agreed. The bank will adopt its normal criteria in deciding whether or not to agree to the customer's request (see Section 8.4) and its decision will be put in writing. Technically all overdrafts are repayable on demand though in reality they are allowed for the period agreed and would not be called in earlier unless there were exceptional circumstances.

The rate of interest on an overdraft is usually fixed in relation to the bank's base rate, i.e. 5 per cent over base rate, and will vary as base rate changes; but there are some accounts on which the rate is fixed for the term of the advance. The advantage of an overdraft, as distinct from a fixed loan, is that the interest is charged only on the fluctuating balance from day-to-day, and therefore the account holder gets the advantage of lower interest charges as amounts are paid in from day-to-day. With a loan account the sum outstanding remains constant until repayments are made by transfer from the customer's current account to his loan account, and hence the interest charges are higher. However, there will almost certainly be commission charges on the current account because the account is overdrawn, whereas if the account was kept in credit and the borrowing taken by way of a separate loan account, commission charges might be avoided. Another disadvantage of an overdraft, as compared with a loan, is that with the latter both the customer and the bank know how the borrowing stands. With an overdraft the customer must ensure that the outstanding debit balance is gradually reduced and this is less easy to achieve when sums are coming into the account (salary payments perhaps) and payments going out to meet living expenses. However, with good management of his affairs the customer should be able to achieve the objective of repaying the overdraft on schedule and, if he does so, is more likely to receive favourable treatment if he requests a further overdraft in future.

Budget accounts

The purpose of a budget account is to enable the customer to spread his household expenditure evenly over the 12 months of the year. It is necessary for him to add up all his estimated bills for the year and divide the total by 12 to calculate the amount he needs to pay into the account each month by standing order from his current account. The customer is credited with interest on credit balances and debited with interest in respect of overdrawn amounts plus a commission charge for the work involved. The customer uses a special budget account cheque book.

Personal instalment loans

This term is used to mean the type of loan which is repayable by fixed monthly instalments which include an element of both interest and principal. This is distinct from the ordinary loan account on which interest is debited to the customer's current account quarterly and agreed sums in repayment are debited to his account at fixed intervals. Personal loans are for sums of £500 or more and for a declared specific purpose, such as the purchase of a car, house improvement, etc. The nominal rate of interest appears relatively low but, as it is charged on the whole sum borrowed for the whole period of the loan even though repayments are made regularly, the APR will work out at a rate well above the normal rate on an overdraft. The interest for the whole period is added to the principal sum and the total of the two divided by the number of months for which the loan is granted to work out the amount of the monthly repayment instalment.

Despite the relatively high cost to the borrower, personal instalment loans offer several advantages to the borrower:

1   The interest payable is no higher than that payable on a hire-purchase agreement and there is no arrangement whereby the goods can be claimed by the lender as they can under such an agreement
2   No security is required as there might be for an overdraft or ordinary loan
3   The rate of interest is fixed for the whole term of the loan, hence the amount of the monthly instalments is agreed at the outset and the borrower is able to budget for them
4   Usually the outstanding debt is covered by free life insurance, thus protecting the bank as well as the relatives of the borrower in the event of his death; furthermore, it is customary to include unemployment and sickness cover, but the borrower has to pay for this

Term loans

Banks offer a number of products that come under this category, the most common being the house improvement loan. They are invariably secured loans and are usually for sums of £10,000 or more for a specific purpose. The most common type of security is a second mortgage on the customer's house but it could be against an insurance policy or stocks and shares.

The loan is for a fixed period of years and will specify the number and timing of repayment instalments. Some types of loan attract a fixed rate of interest but the more usual arrangement is for a variable rate of interest related to base rate.

House mortgages

The banks are very much involved in lending to house buyers against mortgages on their houses and offer strong competition to the building societies who at one time were regarded as the main source for this type of finance. The property is charged to the bank by a full legal mortgage (though in rare instances the bank will take an equitable mortgage which gives a less satisfactory charge over the property). If the borrower defaults on his repayments the bank could repossess the house, sell it and credit the customer's account with any excess monies after the outstanding mortgage and the expenses have been accounted for. In the event of there being insufficient proceeds, the outstanding amount remains as a debt payable by the customer to the bank.

Mortgages are usually for a long period of years, the most common period being 25 years. Over this period the customer repays the loan by monthly instalments which include interest as well as principal, but only interest if the mortgage is an endowment type (see below). The interest is variable and is adjusted in line with changes in bank base rates, and tax relief is given on the interest on the first £30,000 of the home loan at the basic rate of 25 per cent (possibly 40 per cent if the customer is in that income tax bracket).

There are two types of house mortgage, the repayment mortgage and the endowment mortgage. Under the former, the borrower repays a fixed amount each month to cover interest and principal with most of each instalment covering interest in the earlier years of the mortgage, but the interest element decreases year by year and in the last few years of the mortgage nearly all of the instalment comprises capital repayment. The endowment type of mortgage is related to an endowment insurance policy covering the principal sum and, upon maturity of the policy (which coincides with the end of the mortgage period), the principal is paid off from the proceeds of the policy. During the life of the policy the customer pays the insurance premiums to the insurance company and the interest to the bank on the amount of the mortgage. The endowment mortgage offers security both to the customer's next of kin and to the bank should he die during the term of the mortgage. If the endowment policy is of the 'with profits' type the customer benefits from sharing in the profits of the insurance company and the declared profits are payable in addition to the insured sum upon maturity of the policy.

Another type of mortgage is the pension mortgage. This is of benefit to the customer who is able to convert part of his pension from his employer, or from a private pension scheme, into a lump sum upon retirement up to a maximum of 25 per cent of the pension. In anticipation of this, the pension mortgage allows part of the principal sum to be covered by the lump sum to be received upon retirement, whilst the rest is covered by an endowment policy. Hence the customer pays pension contributions which can be offset against income tax, insurance premiums and the interest to the bank on the whole of the principal sum of the mortgage.

Other types of mortgage are available that are tied to unit trusts and PEPs (personal equity plans) (see p. 40). The mortgages are repaid from the sale of the unit trust units on the one hand and the sale of the stocks and shares in the PEP on the other.

Bridging loans

It is not always possible to synchronise the sale and purchase of houses so that the proceeds of the sale of one will pay for the purchase of the other, with maybe a new higher mortgage. The banks are usually able to help bridge the gap provided that the customer has genuinely sold his existing house and the bank may well want contracts exchanged on it before it is willing to temporarily finance the purchase of the new house. When purchasing a house it is usual to pay a deposit (usually 5 per cent these days, whereas it used to be 10 per cent) when contracts are exchanged. This deposit is non-returnable should the buyer not fulfil the contract. The bank will advance this deposit, if necessary, as part of the bridging arrangement, and then advance the remaining 95 per cent on completion of the purchase. Upon completion of the sale the net proceeds are credited to the customer's account and the advance paid off. This assumes of course that the customer has made adequate provision for the extra finance required, if he is going up market, by a new and higher mortgage from the bank (or elsewhere) and has allowed himself a sufficient margin to pay all the legal and other costs involved in the sale and purchase. The bank will have to satisfy itself about this point before agreeing to the bridging loan.

What has been described so far is a **closed bridging loan** where there has been exchange of contracts on the sale before the purchase is financed. This is relatively safe as far as the bank is concerned, but there is the remote chance that the buyer of the customer's house may not fulfil his contract and it will be necessary to find another buyer and at, possibly, a lower price. However the customer should be able to retain the 5 per cent deposit.

If the bank is sufficiently satisfied about a customer's creditworthiness it might agree to **open bridging finance**, but this is very risky and therefore not popular with the banks, especially during a housing slump. What is involved here is the purchase of the new property before the old one is sold. The bank may have the deeds of both properties as security unless the old house is mortgaged elsewhere, but the sale may be protracted and the cost of servicing the debt (i.e. interest payments) could prove too much for the borrower.

8.4   The Principles of Lending

When a bank receives a request for an advance there are a number of questions that must be considered, and many that must be asked of the customer before it is in a position to make a decision as to whether to lend the money or not (or to make a recommendation if the request has to be sent to an area office). Some of the questions will not be difficult to answer if the customer has been known for years and the bank is therefore aware of how well or badly the customer has managed his finances in the past. If the customer is a relatively new one, however, the banker may well have to ask some searching questions in order to be satisfied that if the money is lent there is every likelihood that it will be repaid, and in the time agreed. These questions are usually answered these days on the detailed form which the customer has to complete when making the application for the advance from which a credit score will be calculated. Let us look at each of these basic considerations in turn.

How much, for what purpose, and for how long?

Obviously the customer must indicate how much he wants to borrow and why he needs the money. He should also be able to give a good indication of the term of the advance, i.e. how long it will be before the advance is repaid. The bank is going to be happier with the proposition if the customer has worked out requirements in a businesslike fashion, and can demonstrate quite clearly how the flow of funds is going to affect borrowing needs (during the first year and, preferably, beyond that). If the customer is vague about requirements, and virtually leaves the bank manager to do the calculations, he is not creating confidence and may well have the request rejected simply on the basis that he lacks perception as to what the advance is going to mean in terms of setting aside sufficient funds each year to service the debt, and to repay some of it.

However succinctly the customer has put together the proposition, it may still be necessary to ask searching questions in order to decide whether or not the customer is likely to achieve his plans. If the advance is a straightforward one for the purchase of a car, or to modernise a kitchen or something of that nature, the bank has to look at the customer's income to consider whether or not he is likely to repay as quickly as suggested. The personal loan application form requires the customer to fill in details of both his income and his basic expenditure and it is necessary to verify the figures given if at all possible.

How, and when, is the advance to be repaid?

It may be easy for the customer to borrow money, but repayment can often turn out to be more difficult than expected. The bank will want the advance to be reduced from month to month or from year to year, and for the customer to demonstrate how this is going to be achieved.

There are exceptions to the principle of gradual reduction, of course. The borrower may, for instance, require an advance in anticipation of receiving a lump sum which will completely repay the borrowing. If it is to come from, say, the maturity of an insurance policy, the bank may require the customer to sign an instruction to the insurance company that the funds should be paid direct to the bank. Each application must be judged on its merits, of course, but what must be clear at the outset is the **source** of repayment. What the bank will want to avoid is a dormant loan or overdraft, and therefore it will need to examine very carefully the customer's ability to make the expected reductions and to pay the interest.

Creditworthiness

'Creditworthiness' really means 'Is the customer a suitable person to borrow from the bank?'. In other words, it calls for an assessment of **character**, and this is something which the bank manager has to do from the customer's past history and/or by making judicious enquiries. The manager will know, for instance, whether the customer has borrowed from the bank before (and, if so, whether he repaid on time and without any difficulties from the bank's point of view). Also whether the customer has run the account in a satisfactory manner. Have cheques ever been returned through lack of funds? Has a reasonable balance been maintained; an active account operated? What have been the sources of income? Has the account ever been overdrawn without prior arrangement? What is known about the customer's personal assets – does he own his own house and what securities has he lodged for safe custody?

If the customer is a new one, it may be necessary to make enquiries from a previous bank, or through a credit-reporting agency.

The customer's account may help in forming an opinion as to whether or not he lives beyond his existing means and the manager may know his customer socially, or through business contacts and thus have built up a picture. If the customer is known to have only modest means yet drives around in a very expensive car and generally appears to be living extravagantly, the manager may well doubt his suitability for an advance.

Security for an advance

If a borrower is prepared to lodge some security for an advance, the bank is more likely to agree to it (or more likely to agree to lend a larger sum than would otherwise be forthcoming). However, the bank does not want to rely on the security, in the sense that the last thing it will want to do is to **foreclose**. The security is there as a last resort, and therefore the bank will look just as closely at the facts and figures concerning the source of repayment as it would do if no security was to be lodged. By no means all advances are secured, instead they may be based entirely on the creditworthiness of the borrower, but obviously the bank is going to be happier if there is security to fall back on should some event, such as unemployment or illness, occur. Quite often the best form of security is an insurance policy covering such an event or events.

SCRAP: a useful acronym

The above comments will, I trust, have built up a picture of what the bank must look for when considering an application for an advance. A number of acronyms have been suggested to help the student to remember these basic considerations and I hope the following will be useful to you:

- **S**ecurity
- **C**reditworthiness
- **R**epayment
- **A**mount and Term
- **P**urpose

Remember that **SCRAP** is nothing more than an aide-memoire and you must be able to explain what these terms mean. Furthermore the acronym does not place the basic considerations in their best order of importance which would more likely be Amount and Term, Purpose, Creditworthiness, Repayment, Security.

Review Questions

1　What is the purpose of a current account? What are the three main facilities that it offers? (8.2)
2　What is meant by a high interest cheque account? (8.2)
3　How would you distinguish between tiered and banded rates of interest? (8.2)
4　What are the advantages of a gold account? (8.2)
5　What are savings accounts? Can cheques be drawn on them? (8.2)
6　How would you distinguish between a savings account and an investment account? (8.2)
7　How can money be invested in the London Money Market? (8.2)
8　What is a certificate of deposit? (8.2)
9　What is meant by TESSA accounts? How do they operate? (8.2)
10　Why do people save? List and explain the main reasons. (8.2)
11　Which factors must be taken into consideration by the saver in deciding what account to place his funds in? (8.2)
12　What is meant by an overdraft? (8.3)
13　How can one compare an overdraft with a loan from the point of view of cost? (8.3)
14　What is a budget account? Why would a customer wish to open one? (8.3)
15　How would you distinguish between a personal instalment loan and an ordinary loan account? (8.3)
16　What are the advantages to the borrower of a personal instalment loan? (8.3)
17　What is meant by a term loan? (8.3)
18　How would you distinguish between a repayment mortgage and an endowment mortgage? (8.3)
19　What is a pension mortgage? (8.3)
20　How would you distinguish between a closed bridging loan and an open bridging loan? Which is the more risky, and why? (8.3)
21　Using an acronym, explain the considerations that must be taken into account when an application for an advance is received. (8.4)
22　Why should a bank find it needs to 'foreclose' on a customer's borrowing? (8.4)

┌───

— **Past Examination Questions** ——————————

1 (a) Describe the reasons why people save. Give examples in your
       answer.   (*6 marks*)

   (b) Explain the principles banks follow when considering a lending
       application.   (*12 marks*)

   (c) Banks act as a link between borrowers and savers. What is this
       called?   (*2 marks*)

2 Terry Rist is 41 years old, married with two children. He works as a car
   salesman and last year earned £16,000. His wife works part-time in an
   estate agent's office earning £80 per week. The Rists have lived in their
   present house for 12 years and they bought it from the council 8 years
   ago for £15,000. The mortgage is with your bank.
   The Rists are very careful with their money and have saved £2,000 in a
   building society. They have also bought shares in all the recent pri-
   vatisations, e.g. British Telecom, British Gas and the regional water
   authorities.
   They want to borrow £5,000 to pay for their eldest daughter's wedding
   and repay it over 5 years. You know that their second daughter is also
   engaged to be married.
   The Rists have had several loans from you in the past and have always
   repaid them. The loan over 5 years will cost them about £130 per
   month.
   Briefly explain the principles on which you would make a decision on
   whether to lend the money and show how the Rists meet these principles. You do not need to make any calculations.   (*20 marks*)

3 Which bank lending service would you recommend to meet each of the
   following needs? Briefly explain the service and give two advantages
   and two disadvantages for each service:
   (a) A customer wants a loan for five months, to be available to meet
       possible expenses which may be incurred before the receipt of
       income.   (*7 marks*)

   (b) A householder wants to build a porch costing £2,500 onto the front
       of her house.   (*7 marks*)

   (c) A customer wants to spread the payment of irregular bills through-
       out the year.   (*8 marks*)

9   Other bank services

9.1   Introduction

In this chapter we will examine in detail the main services of the banks to personal customers apart from those of accepting deposits and providing loans and overdrafts.

In order to understand the banks' services better it is desirable to know the structure of their balance sheets. These accounts also help to explain their role in society.

9.2   Personal Services

Money transmission and payment services

We have already looked at the various methods of payment that the banks provide for their customers and the ways in which funds can be transmitted, in Chapters 6 and 7, and the reader should refer back to those chapters. It is appropriate to mention them at this juncture as they are important services which the banks provide, third in importance perhaps to the two main services of accepting deposits and lending money.

Status enquiries

The personal account holder may from time to time have occasion to make a status enquiry concerning an individual or firm with which he is going to have dealings. He may, for instance, be letting furnished accommodation, and would need to have some assurance concerning the tenant's ability to pay the rent and, if possible, concerning respectability. He needs to ascertain the name and branch of that person's bank and pass the information to his bank with an indication of the amount of the rent. The reply from the tenant's bank will be a guarded and unsigned one, but it should help the customer to decide whether to go ahead or not. As we saw in Chapter 4, the banks must be very careful in divulging information about their customers' affairs, but there is an implied consent that they may answer status enquiries from other banks and, since the Jack Report, they have tended to ask their customer to sign a statement that they have no objection to the bank answering such enquiries.

Safe custodies

Customers with deeds and share certificates may deposit them with the bank for safe custody and other valuables may be deposited in a locked deed box or sealed up in a parcel. Boxes and parcels are numbered by the bank to identify them, and receipts are issued which usually state 'Contents Unknown'. The bank does not want to know the contents, and usually advises the customer to take out appropriate insurance. The banks tend now to charge for safe custody services and thus are paid bailees (but, as we saw in Chapter 4, their legal position may well be unaffected by the fact that they are no longer gratuitous bailees).

Stocks and shares

The purchase of stocks and shares is likely to be of interest to personal rather than business customers, and those who wish to buy or sell may ask the bank to arrange it. The bank will pass on the order to a securities dealer which, in the case of the larger retail banks, will be a member company of its own group of companies, unless the customer specifies that he wants the transaction to go through another dealer. If the customer wants advice on investing in a particular company or in a particular sector, the bank will pass the request to its securities dealer, unless the amount of money to be invested justifies an approach to one of the bank's financial advisers who would be willing to talk to the customer about his investments in general. As we saw in Chapter 4, under SIB regulations a bank must choose between giving independent financial advice about financial services and selling only their own financial services.

A bank will look after a customer's investment portfolio for an annual management charge, and, if the customer is willing to give it the authority, will buy and sell securities as it considers appropriate in order to maintain or improve the income and/or capital value of the investments.

Some of the banks are involved in Personal Equity Plans (PEP) and offer this service to customers who invest in stocks and shares and unit trusts. Investments in PEP are free of income tax and capital gains tax (see p. 40).

Travel facilities

Customers who are travelling abroad may obtain a supply of foreign currency-(ies) and travellers' cheques from the bank (see Figure 9.1). The travellers' cheques are made out in convenient denominations of sterling or foreign currency and, being drawn on a reputable international bank, will be readily encashed at banks abroad. They are signed by the customer in front of an officer of the bank before he takes them away and, when encashing them abroad, the customer must sign them again in front of a cashier in order that the two signatures can be compared. Similarly, if he cashes a travellers' cheque at a hotel abroad, he must sign it when doing so. Lost cheques may be stopped by notifying the issuing bank.

As an alternative to, in or addition to, travellers' cheques, the customer may use a book of Eurocheques and a special cheque guarantee card, both of them supplied by his bank, but he is not able to use his ordinary cheque guarantee card. If he has a bank gold card he would be able to obtain foreign currency from those banks abroad that are members of the Mastercard or Visa organisation (whichever applies), and an ordinary credit card bearing the symbol of either of those organisations could also be used to obtain finance or to buy goods abroad.

He could also arrange travel insurance through the bank's insurance department.

Insurance services

In addition to the travel insurance mentioned above, the bank's insurance department or specialised subsidiary company would be able to offer the whole range of insurance facilities, including the type of insurance cover that may be required when taking out a mortgage and ordinary life insurance cover, investment bonds, etc. Banks also sell personal pension plans through their insurance subsidiaries.

Executor and trustee services

The larger banks have departments that cater for the needs of those customers making a will or, possibly, proving a will. They will act as executor and, if appropriate, trustee of a will and relieve the customer of the problem of finding a relative or friend who is willing to take on the task.

Figure 9.1　Travel facilities

Income tax services

This department will undertake to prepare and submit an income tax return and, hopefully, by being more knowledgeable about the allowances that can be claimed, save more in tax than the cost of the bank's services.

Estate agencies

During the housing boom of the 1980s, two of the banks (Lloyds and TSB) became involved in the estate agency business, as did Abbey National. As they are also providers of home loans, they are able to tie up the two types of business, offering mortgage finance to those customers to whom they sell houses, as well as to customers generally. If a bank customer buys a house through the bank's estate agency and takes out a mortgage from the bank, the bank is in a better position to control all the financial transactions involved and to chase up the seller of the property if there is a delay. If the customer is both buying and selling and bridging finance is required, this too could be in the hands of the bank.

9.3   Balance Sheet of a Retail Bank

By looking at the balance sheet of a large retail bank we can tell a great deal about its activities – in particular its sources of funds and how these funds are employed to make a profit. The large international banks are part of a banking group with the retail bank as the central parent company. For our purposes we need look only at the balance sheet of the retail bank and not at the balance sheet for the group as a whole. If you are employed in a bank, you would be wise to look at your own bank's balance sheet, examining the group's balance sheet to discover the nature of the subsidiary companies, but paying particular attention to the balance sheet of the parent bank itself. Look carefully at the explanatory notes accompanying the balance sheet and read through the chairman's report or statement which will no doubt give you additional information about the bank's activities.

Like any company's balance sheet, a bank's balance sheet shows the position at a particular date – usually 31 December – and the figures relating to the previous year are shown side by side with the current figures. Unlike an ordinary company's balance sheet, however, the assets are shown in the opposite order – instead of showing the fixed assets (e.g. Premises) first, these are shown last and the liquid assets (commencing with Cash in Hand, the most liquid of all) are shown first.

Let us now examine in turn the liabilities and assets of our simplified specimen balance sheet in Figure 9.2. The liabilities will show us the sources from which the bank has obtained its funds, and the assets will show us how these funds have been used by the bank to make a profit.

XYZ BANK
Balance Sheet as at 31 December 1992

	£ Million		£ Million
Capital and Reserves	2,500	Cash and Balances at the Bank of England	700 8,000
Loan Capital	1,000	Money at Call and Short Notice	1,000
Deposits	50,000	Bills Discounted	1,000
		Cheques in Course of Collection	1,000
		Best peak's of Deposit	800
		Investments	1,000
		Advances	40,000
		Premises	1,000
	53,500		53,500

Figure 9.2   Simplified retail bank balance sheet

9.4   Liabilities

Capital and reserves

The first item on the liabilities side in a bank's balance sheet is similar to that found in any company's balance sheet, i.e. Capital and Reserves. The ordinary capital represents the amount subscribed by the ordinary shareholders. There may also be preference capital – this is subscribed capital that is entitled to a fixed rate of dividend which has to be paid before ordinary shareholders receive any dividend. The reserves are there as a result of retaining some of the profits over the years, and from the revaluation of bank premises as these values have appreciated with increases in property values generally over the long period of years that the bank has been in existence. Whilst these two items amount to very large sums of money in themselves, they are nevertheless small as a proportion of total liabilities, whereas in the balance sheet of an ordinary industrial or commercial company these shareholders' funds would account for a large part of the total liabilities. This arises from the fact that the bank has one enormous liability – customers' deposits – which is peculiar to a deposit-taking institution.

Loan capital

This is capital that has been **borrowed**, as distinct from shareholders' funds which have been **subscribed** and which represent the shareholders' ownership of the company. Those who lend capital are not shareholders, and have no say in the running of the bank. They receive an agreed rate of interest on the capital which is lent to the bank for a set period of years.

Deposits

This colossal item represents the deposits which the bank has accepted – both from its retail customers and through the wholesale money market – plus a relatively small amount relating to its own internal accounts. The ratio of current accounts to savings and investment accounts varies, depending primarily on the rates of interest paid on savings and investment accounts; when these are high, customers are tempted to transfer from current accounts to the more profitable accounts, whereas when they are low, they tend to keep larger balances on their current accounts.

9.5 Assets

Cash on hand and balances with the Bank of England

A bank's most liquid asset is the cash it has in its tills and strong rooms, and it must ensure that it has sufficient available to meet its customers' demand at any time. Balances at the Bank of England are almost as good as cash in that they can be drawn upon to provide additional notes and coin very quickly, and also can be used to make payments between the banks themselves. An international bank would also keep balances with state banks abroad for the same purposes – to enable it to obtain additional notes and coin, and also to settle transactions with other banks.

The banks use their current account balances with the Bank of England to settle the transactions with one another at the Bankers' Clearing House, as well as transactions with the Bank of England itself. Such balances are also a vital reserve which must be kept in order to be able to meet its day-to-day needs, especially the demands for withdrawal in cash from its customers. The Bank of England requires all of the banks to submit balance sheets and other returns to it each month, as it is empowered to do within its supervisory role (see p. 22), and when examining these would be quick to react if it felt that a particular bank was not keeping sufficient cash. There will always be an inclination to keep only the minimum of cash and balances at the Bank of England because they produce no income. In addition to its operational account at the Bank, the banks are obliged to keep a balance on a separate no-operational account with the Bank of England equal to around half of 1 per cent of its eligible liabilities (that is, its short-term sterling deposits).

Cheques in course of collection

Because as far as the bank is concerned the cheque clearing process takes 3 working days, a bank will always have at any particular time an appreciable amount of money owed to it by other banks in respect of cheques which have yet to be cleared. In Figure 9.2 this amounts to £1,000 million, and this is a lot of money to have 'idle', in the sense that it is earning no income. At first sight these funds would appear to be very liquid in that they will be received within a few days and therefore their total could be included amongst the bank's liquid assets. This is not so, however, because there will be cheques in the process of being cleared that are **claims against the bank** – i.e. cheques drawn on it by customers and made payable to customers of other banks. We must assume that these amount to something like the £1,000 million of cheques drawn on other banks, and therefore if the banks were to close for a few days and clear all outstanding claims this item would disappear from the balance sheet. Clearly, therefore, Cheques in Course of Collection should not be regarded as a liquid asset, and in the past when official liquidity ratios and reserve ratios have been in force this asset has not been included in determining how liquid the bank is.

Money at call and short notice

This asset comprises money lent overnight (or at the most on up to 14 days' notice), mostly to the London discount houses, but also to money brokers, discount brokers, stockdealers and bullion brokers. Next to cash, this is the bank's most liquid asset. Most of it can be called in next day, and the size of it will reflect the bank's needs for that day. If it expects heavy withdrawals by its customers and other needs for cash – i.e. from cash on hand and balances at the Bank of England – then it will run down its money at call to provide the extra cash required. This asset produces an income to the bank, but the rates of interest received will vary with market conditions, though on average they will be **relatively** low to reflect the fact that the funds are highly liquid. When funds are short on the money market, the banks are able to demand relatively high rates. Most of the funds lent to the money market are secured by the lodgement of government stocks and bills of exchange. The activities of the banks in providing funds for the discount houses thus affect the gilt-edged and bill markets, and in order to protect the efficient functioning of these markets the banks are expected to hold a reasonable proportion of their eligible liabilities in secured advances to the discount houses each day.

Bills discounted

Included under this heading are Treasury bills and commercial bills of exchange which the bank has discounted, usually with the intention of hold-ing them to maturity. The discount charged when buying commercial bills represents the interest the bank receives on this asset, and this will vary with market conditions, but tends to be somewhat higher than the bank's base rate. The banks buy the Treasury bills from the discount houses after they have held them for at least a week, and the rate of interest on these bills is determined at the weekly tender (see p. 24), and tends to be around $1/2$ per cent below the bank's base rates. They are 91-day bills, and the commercial bills are usually 3-month or 6-month bills, though some may be of longer term.

Certificates of deposit

As we saw on p. 125, certificates of deposit certify that a sum of money has been deposited with a bank for a specified length of time. They are usually for substan-tial amounts in sterling (or possibly US dollars), in multiples of £10,000 with a minimum of £50,000 and, normally, a maximum of £500,000. The sum deposited is repayable to bearer at a prescribed date, and it attracts interest at an agreed rate which is indicated on the certificate. As a certificate of deposit is negotiable by simple delivery; it can easily be sold at the market price for certificates of deposit on the day it is sold. The price paid will reflect the current rates of interest in the money market generally for the outstanding term until maturity. As we are look-ing at the assets side of the balance sheet, this item must represent certificates of deposit which the bank has acquired – that is certificates issued by other banks. When they mature they will be presented to the banks concerned for repayment. Any certificates issued by the bank whose balance sheet is illustrated in Figure 9.2, will be included as liabilities under the item Current, Deposit and Other Accounts.

Investments

These are in the main investments in government and government-backed stocks. They are of various maturity dates, and the bank will have purchased them so as to ensure that it has portfolios of stocks maturing at regular intervals, as well as some long-dated stocks which will produce a good return well into the future. These stocks produce a better income for the bank than any of the assets con-sidered so far, but the precise yield must depend upon the price paid for them, as well as the rate of interest paid on them.

Advances

This is by far the biggest asset, and the most profitable to the bank. It includes overdrafts and loans of all types – for example, straightforward loans to individuals and firms, personal instalment loans, term loans to industry, mortgage loans and export loans. It also includes a large sum of money placed in the wholesale money markets for periods exceeding 1 month.

On the majority of these advances the rate of interest charged will be related to the bank's base rate or to LIBOR (London Inter-Bank Offered Rate), and quoted as such, possibly ranging from 1 per cent above for large industrial customers to 5 per cent or more above for the private borrower. On fixed-term loans the rate will be quoted as a specific rate per cent, such as on a mortgage. On personal instalment loan, the rate is fixed for the whole term of the loan and is charged on the whole amount for the whole term of the loan despite the fact that the advance is repaid in monthly instalments and the average outstanding loan is only half the sum advanced. The true rate of interest is thus approximately twice the nominal rate charged to the customer, as is usually the case with hire-purchase contracts. A prudent banker must always provide for the fact that some of its advances may never be repaid, and thus the provision for bad and doubtful debts will have been deducted from the total of advances. During periods of recession, when a high number of firms and companies run into difficulties, the banks will of course make bigger provisions for bad debts.

Premises

This asset consists of all of the bank's premises and equipment after allowance for depreciation and amortisation.

9.6   What Does the Balance Sheet Tell Us About Bank Services?

On the liabilities side, the item Current, Deposit and Other Accounts reflects one of the bank's main services – the acceptance of deposits on current, savings and investment accounts.

On the assets side, Cash on Hand is necessary if the bank is to be able to provide the service of supplying notes and coin as and when required by its customers. Cheques in course of collection are cheques which have been paid in by customers, and which the bank is clearing on their behalf. The cheques payments mechanism is a vital service which the banks provide. The provision of Money at Call is an essential service to the money market, and to the authorities in carrying out their monetary policy. Similarly in purchasing and holding Treasury bills the banks are providing funds for the government, and assist the authorities further in pursuing their monetary policy.

The other part of the asset Bills Discounted – the commercial bills which have been discounted – represents another vital service to the bank's customers. By discounting bills for them the bank is in fact providing short-term finance in anticipation of the receipt of the proceeds at maturity of the bills. This is a particularly important service for exporters. The bank's Investments are mainly in the public sector and here again the banks are providing a service to both central and local government, enabling them to acquire necessary finance – and also, as far as central government is concerned, to carry out its fiscal and monetary policies.

The provision of credit to customers in the form of overdrafts and loans of various types is reflected in the item Advances.

Figure 9.2 shows that the shareholders' and depositors' funds are invested by the bank in a variety of ways. Some of the assets are held because they are liquid (i.e. are either in the form of cash or could be fairly easily turned into cash), and some are invested longer-term in gilt-edged stocks, but the majority are lent out to produce the highest possible return in the form of advances.

A bank has the difficult task of striking a balance between using its borrowed funds in a liquid fashion in order to able to repay its depositors on demand or within the period of notice required on the particular type of account, and investing them in longer-term – and hence more profitable – ways. The high returns from lending enable a bank to meet its shareholders' expectations of a good dividend and a build-up of sound reserves, but the proportion of deposits invested in this way must be limited in order to stay sufficiently liquid. Experience has helped in striking the balance, of course, particularly the experience of those banks which have run into difficulties in the past in meeting depositors' demands for repayment and which have had to close their doors (or have been helped to survive by other banks). Another important factor which these difficulties have highlighted is that not only must the proportion of deposits lent out as advances be limited, but also that the advances themselves must be spread over a wide range of industries.

In supervising the banks the Bank of England will look especially carefully at each bank's ratio of liquid assets to deposits and to the way its advances are spread, and will call for some change if it is not satisfied.

As we saw in Chapter 2, the Bank of England holds the Deposit Protection Fund which has been subscribed to by all the banks, and in the event of a bank going into liquidation because it cannot fully repay its depositors, each account holder is guaranteed a repayment of 75 per cent up to a maximum balance of £20,000 i.e. a maximum of repayment of £15,000.

1   What is meant by a status enquiry? (9.2)
2   Why must a bank be careful in answering a status enquiry? (9.2)
3   What types of securities and other items may a customer place on safe custody? (9.2)
4   How can a bank help a customer who wants to buy or sell shares? (9.2)
5   Will a bank manage a customer's portfolio of stocks and shares for him? (9.2)
6   What travel facilities are available to a bank's customer who is going abroad? (9.2)
7   What types of insurance do the banks provide? (9.2)
8   Will a bank act as executor and trustee? (9.2)
9   Will a bank fill in a customer's tax return for him? (9.2)
10   What are the potential advantages to a bank of having its own estate agency? (9.2)
11   What is the main liability of a bank? (9.4)
12   What is the significance of the asset Cash in Hand and Balances with the Bank of England? (9.5)
13   Why is the asset Cheques in Course of Collection not a liquid asset? (9.5)
14   What is Money at call and Short Notice? (9.5)
15   Which two types of bill are included in the asset Bills Discounted? (9.5)
16   What is the source of the certificates of deposit that appear as an asset in a bank's balance sheet? (9.5)
17   What is the nature of a bank's Investments? (9.5)
18   Which items are included under the asset Advances? (9.5)
19   How may the rate of interest on an advance be quoted? (9.5)
20   How are the various bank services reflected in a bank's balance sheet? (9.6)
21   Why must a bank strike a balance between liquidity and profitability? (9.6)

— **Past Examination Question** —

P. Fogg is going on a holiday of about 80 days. He expects to travel around various countries. List **two** options that are available to him to pay his way and give **two** advantages for each option.

Which option would you recommend?   (Part question, *6 marks*)

10 Plastic and electronic banking

┌─ **Chapter objectives** ───┐

When you have carefully studied this chapter you should be able to:
- Explain how the system of telephone and homebanking works
- Define the term EFTPOS and give an account of recent developments
  in connection with it e.g. the introduction of the Switch and Delta
  systems
- Explain the terms 'credit', 'debit', 'charge', 'store' and 'smart' in relation to plastic cards, and list the advantages and disadvantages of each
  of them

└──┘

10.1 Introduction

The banks have deliberately sought ways and means of reducing the use of both
cash and cheques in order to cut down the volume of both cash and paper that
they have to cope with. Cash is expensive to store and to handle and there is considerable risk in having large amounts on the premises and in transporting it from
bank to bank. The volume of cheques that is handled by the Bankers' Clearing
House is enormous, and each cheque has to be handled several times from the
point that it is paid in at a branch of the collecting bank to the point where it is
paid by the paying bank. Labour is expensive and anything that can be done to
reduce the need for it will clearly help the banks' profits.

The transfer of funds by electronic means has proved to be the answer and the
use of plastic cards at the cash point in supermarkets and other retail outlets has
developed very rapidly indeed during the 1990s. It is therefore essential for the
banker to be aware of the various types of plastic cards that are in use and the
ways in which the retailer is able to obtain reimbursement for their use.

Home banking has developed less rapidly but, nevertheless, it has proved
popular not only amongst private account holders but also for the small businessman. There are many home banking systems in existence, and the reader needs to
be aware of what they entail.

Obtaining	balance and/or list of last five entries
Ordering	Cheque book paying-in book statement
Giving instruction about	standing order direct debit transferring from one account to another paying a bill

Figure 10.1   Homebanking

10.2   Telephone and Homebanking

For the person who is unable to get to his bank to carry out transactions or would prefer not to have to do so, a number of banks and building societies now offer a home banking system where all the instructions to the bank are given over the telephone (see Figure 10.1). As an example of this let us take Actionline, the system provided to customers of NatWest. The customer who wishes to participate is provided with a portable tone keypad and information as to code numbers which he can key into his telephone using the keypad, first to identify himself and then to give instructions as to what information he wants or what action(s) he wants the bank to take. He can, if he wishes, identify himself via the keypad and then give verbal requests and instructions. As to the information he may obtain by telephone 24 hours a day and 7 days a week , he can ask for his balance and/or for details of the last five entries on his account, order a cheque book, paying-in book or statement, give standing order and direct debit instructions and transfer money between his current account and any other account he may have with the bank. For regular payments such as electricity or gas bills, the customer can telephone to give details of the accounts to be credited, including the account numbers, sort codes and reference numbers, and then the bank sends an authorisation form for each of the utilities concerned which the customer signs and returns. When a bill is received, he simply notifies the bank by telephone of the amount to be paid.

Coupled with the use of his service card to guarantee cheques, obtain cash through an ATM and to carry out transactions through Switch (see below), it is conceivable that a customer who receives regular credits direct to his account, such as his salary, could run his account without ever visiting the branch. For some banks (e.g. Midland and NatWest) the customer does not even need to order a new cheque book as this is sent to him automatically.

The Bank of Scotland's home banking system (HOBS) operates via the customer's television set through a special keyboard attached to the set, and TSB's Speedlink provides the customer with a link to the bank's computer. Lloyds' system is called Homebank, Girobank's system is DIALOG, Clydesdale's is Telebank and Royal Bank of Scotland's Phoneline. Six building societies run homebanking systems, Nationwide, Halifax, Alliance and Leicester, National and Provincial, Northern Rock and Nottingham building societies.

Midland Bank has a subsidiary company called First Direct which operates the account entirely by post and telephone. The account is opened by post and the customer, in addition to being able to carry out homebanking over the telephone, is issued with a special chequebook and ATM card.

10.3   Debit Cards

The term debit cards is used to mean those bank and building society cards which may be used as a means of payment for goods and which result in debits to the cardholder's account in about 3 days and thus do not provide for a period of credit (see Figure 10.2).

For many years representatives from the banks, large retailers, and British Telecom, negotiated for an EFTPOS (Electronic Funds Transfer Point of Sale) system. The discussions were protracted by controversy as to who should pay for the equipment that would be necessary, especially all the terminals that have to be installed at the tills in the stores. The banks maintained that as the retailers would benefit most, they should pay the lion's share of the costs, whereas the retailers claimed that it was the banks that would benefit most through the replacement to some extent of the costly cheque system with the relatively cheap electronic transfers, and furthermore, the amount of cash handling by the banks would be reduced. In the event, the proposed EFTPOS system in which all the larger banks were to participate got no further than the trial stage and, instead, two separate systems, Switch and Delta, have been introduced.

Figure 10.2   Debit cards

Switch cards are issued by Barclays, Midland, NatWest, Clydesdale, Royal Bank of Scotland, and the Bank of Ireland, and by a considerable number of building societies, most of them through the Stasis system operated by Midland Bank which gives indirect access to Switch.

Delta cards which come under the aegis of the Visa organisation, are issued by Barclays (Connect Card), Lloyds (Payment Card), TSB (Bankcard), Co-operative Bank (Pathfinder Card), Credit Lyonnais (a non-UK bank), and two building societies, Nationwide (Payment Card) and Abbey National (Multifunction Card).

Many of these cards are multipurpose in that they serve as combined ATM, cheque guarantee and Switch or Delta cards, and they may be used to buy goods in shops and other retail outlets that participate in the scheme. The card is 'swiped' through a terminal machine which records the details of the customer's bank account and the amount of the transaction and produces a paper slip giving the details and which the customer has to sign to authorise the transaction. The process at the till takes less time than payment by cheque because the cashier has to carefully inspect a cheque to make sure that it is correctly filled in (even if the payee's name and the amount is printed by the retailer) and also he or she has to write the card number on the back of the cheque if the store is to benefit from the protection offered by the cheque guarantee card. Where a retailer does not have an electronic terminal it is nevertheless possible to use a Delta card with the old paper voucher system that was (and to some extent still is) used for credit card transactions. Switch transactions, on the other hand, are all electronic.

The retailer's claims for payment are processed by what is known as a merchant acquirer, which may be his own bank or a specialist company – all charge for the service. The retailer receives payment on the day he hands over the information on disk or the information is relayed through a telephone link to the merchant acquirer. Or, in the case of the retailer who has no electronic terminal, he may send paper Visa vouchers to his merchant acquirer and be credited with them in the same way that he would submit his credit card vouchers for payment.

The customer's account is debited about 3 working days later. This meets a major criticism of the proposed EFTPOS system which would have credited the retailer and debited the customer on the day of the transaction, and put the customer at a disadvantage compared with using a cheque in that a cheque takes 3 days to be debited to his account. The banks and the retailers want to encourage the use of the electronic means of transfer, not discourage the customers from using the system.

APACS has forecast that by the year 2000 debit cards will account for 8 million payments a day in the UK, compared with only 1million credit card transactions, a clear indication that debit cards are being substituted for cheques, cash and credit cards.

The main advantages to the user of a debit card are as follows:

1   There is no need to carry as much cash about
2   They are convenient to use and provide the user with a record of the transaction on his bank statement with the possibility of more easily controlling his expenditure than if he were using cash
3   It is quicker and less complicated than using cheques
4   In that the debit card is usually a combined ATM card it enables cash to be drawn at a cash point

10.4   Credit Cards

In addition to serving as a means of payment in the same way as debit cards, credit cards enable their holders to obtain credit (see Figure 10.3). When they buy goods or services from a shop, hotel, petrol station, or indeed anyone who is willing to

Figure 10.3   Credit cards

accept the particular credit card, the trader swipes the card through his electronic till, if he has one or, otherwise, prepares the appropriate credit card voucher which he requires the customer to sign to authorise the transaction. Most of the larger stores now have electronic terminals adjacent to, or built into, their tills, which not only record debit card transactions but purchases by credit card as well. As for debit cards, the till prints a paper voucher which the customer is required to sign and his signature is verified with that on the card. Unless the amount of the transaction is within the trader's limit laid down by the credit card company, he must make a telephone call to the company to get the transaction sanctioned by them. Most terminals carry out this check automatically whilst the customer is waiting and he may be oblivious of the fact. The trader obtains reimbursement by transmitting the details of the transactions to a merchant acquirer, usually his bank, or by handing over a disk, containing the information. In the case of a paper voucher transaction, the retailer hands the voucher over to the merchant acquirer. The merchant acquirer charges the retailer a commission for this service. The rate of commission varies and the large retailers have been able to negotiate lower fees for handling their vouchers as they are in a better bargaining position.

The cardholder receives credit for his transaction from the date of it to the time that he reimburses the credit card company. If he elects to pay his monthly account in full soon after it is received and within the specified time stated in the statement, then he will receive that period of credit without being charged interest – a period of 56 days at the most. He may, however, take more credit than this and provided his outstanding borrowing does not exceed the individual credit limit laid down for him by the credit company, he need pay no more each month than a minimum amount stipulated in the statement (normally 5 per cent of the outstanding balance). For this credit he must of course pay interest at the current rate laid down by the credit card issuer.

The British banks use either the Mastercard or the Visa international networks (or both) for their credit cards and the cards bear the symbols of either one of these organisations, which are recognised throughout the world. Of the main banks, Barclays issues its Barclaycard, whilst Lloyds, NatWest and Midland issue Access cards and TSB has its own Trustcard.

In addition to their use to obtain credit when buying goods, credit cards may be used at specified ATMs to obtain immediate cash. Such transactions attract a fee and/or interest charge as they amount to an advance payment.

Whereas at one time no charge was made by the British banks to their customers for credit cards, in 1990 most of them started to charge an annual fee and in consequence the number of credit cards in use fell considerably. Also since 1990 retailers have been permitted to discriminate between customers who offer cash and those who want to use a credit card, by charging more to the credit card holder to reflect the charge that the retailer has to pay to obtain payment through a merchant acquirer.

The advantages to the customer of using a credit card are:

1   There is no need to carry as much cash
2   Payment may be spread over a period
3   Even if payment is made each month when the statement is received, there is a period of credit of up to 56 days
4   Automatic access to credit up to the limit established by the credit card issuer, and hence there is no delay in obtaining the goods
5   Cards are widely accepted both in the UK and abroad
6   Credit cards can be used to obtain cash at ATMs
7   Goods may be ordered by telephone

10.5   Debit vs Credit Cards

The term debit cards is used to mean those bank cards which may be used as a means of payment for goods but result in debits to the cardholder's account and not the provision of a period of credit. Thus the Switch and Delta cards mentioned in Section 9.3 above are debit cards – the customer uses his card at the supermarket and about 3 days later his bank account is debited.

The main point of difference between debit cards and credit cards from the customer's point of view is this fact that a debit card does not provide him with credit whereas a credit card does. With a credit card a separate credit card account is opened and is debited with a transaction in about the same period of time as it takes a debit card transaction to be debited to the customer's current account. However, the credit card holder does not have to pay immediately the credit card account is debited. Instead he is sent a statement of account once a month and he has to pay all or an agreed proportion of the outstanding sum by the end of the month. This gives him up to 56 days' free credit if he pays off the balance in full, and several months' credit if he pays off the minimum amount laid down by the credit card company when the account is opened. The credit card provides the cardholder with credit up to a prescribed limit, whereas a debit card can be used by the cardholder for purchases up to the amount of the balance on his current account.

The procedure for the retailer involved with both debit and credit cards is very similar if he has an electronic terminal which will record the transaction when the card is swiped and produce a paper voucher for the customer to sign. However, if the retailer carries out his transactions manually, he will not be able to accept Switch cards because the system is not geared up for paper transactions. However, the Visa organisation will accept Delta transactions on paper vouchers. Credit card transactions may be recorded either electronically or by paper vouchers.

Again from the retailer's point of view, the advantages of both credit and debit card transactions are very similar. In both cases the cards:

1   Provide him with immediate payment
2   Reduce the amount of cash he has to handle and therefore increase security
3   Stimulate sales
4   Save time at the check out vis-à-vis the use of cheques (if he has the means to record the transaction electronically)
5   Provide for transactions beyond the store's limit to be sanctioned, and thus they are not strictly limited in the way that they are where a cheque guarantee card is used
6   Attract lower bank charges than paper (cheque) transactions
7   Reduce the amount of paperwork

10.6   Charge Cards

Charge cards are very similar to debit cards in that they are used to pay for goods and no credit is allowed, but the customer's account is not debited 3 days later. Instead he is sent a monthly account which must be settled within about 25 days. In addition he is charged an enrolment fee and an annual fee and his membership

Figure 10.4   Store card

of the organisation (for example American Express or Diners Club), entitles him to a number of special facilities. His card is well known internationally and will be accepted by airlines and hotels without limit.

The gold cards issued by large retail banks in the UK bear a very close resemblance to charge cards but with the added possibility of an automatic overdraft on special terms (see p. 124).

10.7   Store Cards

Store cards are issued by large retail stores such as Marks and Spencer, House of Fraser, and Harrods (see Figure 10.4). They are very similar to credit cards, but the latter term is usually restricted to cards issued by banks. The customer is sent a monthly statement which he may settle in full or, if he chooses, take credit up to a personal limit laid down by the store with the proviso that he must pay the minimum laid down on the statement (usually 5 per cent). The use of the card is however restricted to branches of the store issuing the card, and the rates of interest charged by the stores tend to be higher than those charged on credit cards.

The cardholder has some privileges over the ordinary customer at the store in that he may receive a special discount on his purchases, especially during sales, and will be invited to previews of sales. Some of the stores that issue store cards will not accept Access and Visa cards and thus the holder of a store card will have the additional advantage of obtaining credit whereas ordinary customers do not.

There is no doubt that the availability of store cards attracts customers to the store and will encourage them to buy goods there rather than elsewhere. Against this advantage to the store must be offset the cost of providing the plastic cards and running the accounts.

Some of the larger stores also compete with the banks in other ways as well as by the issue of plastic cards. Their financial services include personal loans, unit trusts and PEP, insurance and pensions services and even mortgages.

10.8   Smart Cards

Smart card is the name given to a type of charge card which has a microchip built into it containing the personal identity number (PIN number) of the holder, and it can hold large amounts of data including details of the holder's bank accounts and transactions on those accounts. It can identify the holder by recognising the PIN number and also authorise a transaction without the need to refer to a central computer. However, smart cards are costly and entail the installation of new card reading terminals. They have therefore not as yet proved very popular with banks in the UK, but they do afford better security against fraud and may yet be introduced on a wide scale for that reason.

Review Questions

1   What is meant by the term home banking? (10.2)
2   Can standing order payments be made by telephone? (10.2)
3   Can a homebanking system be operated via a domestic television screen? (10.2)
4   What is meant by the term EFTPOS? (10.3)
5   How can a Switch or Delta card be used to settle a transaction at a supermarket? (10.3)
6   What is a credit card? Who is it issued by? (10.4)
7   Do banks charge retailers for collecting credit card payments? (10.4)
8   To what extent can a credit card holder obtain credit even if he settles his monthly statement in full? (10.4)
9   How much of the outstanding amount on the monthly statement must a credit card holder normally pay as a minimum? (10.4)
10   Do the British banks charge their customers for credit cards? (10.4)
11   How would you distinguish between a debit card and a credit card? (10.5)
12   What is a charge card? How does it differ from a debit card? (10.6)
13   What is a store card? How may one be advantageous to the holder? (10.7)
14   What is a smart card? (10.8)

Past Examination Questions

1   Petrol stations say that they could reduce the price of petrol by 1.5 per cent if customers did not pay by credit card. Why should this be?

(2 marks)

Explain the advantages and disadvantages for both retailer and customer of using credit cards.

(18 marks)

2   Plastic cards are playing an increasing role in 'banking'. Explain the use and operation of **three** different types of **bank**-issued plastic cards and list two advantages of each type.

(20 marks)

3   You have been asked by your manager to write a talk to be given to some local store managers explaining the differences between credit and debit cards, how they work and **four** advantages for the retailer of using these cards. Prepare an outline for the talk.

(20 marks)

11 Assessing customer needs

11.1 Introduction

It is of course very important that the banker should be able to listen to his customer's request for assistance, or to seek out his customer to offer him or her services in the light of his (her) circumstances. The banker must be able to assimilate all the facts about the customer's financial and other circumstances and assess what bank services (or services of another financial institution) would best fill his needs. He must then be able to get across to the customer the main features of the service he is offering and, in particular, the advantages of the service to the customer.

Many of the questions in the *Business of Banking* examination paper for the ACIB Banking Certificate are concerned with this topic, and therefore in this chapter we shall look at a number of such questions and the suggested answers to them in the hope that it will help the reader to master the technique of analysing the facts and coming up with the right recommendations. We will look at the circumstances of particular types of customers as they might be expressed in examination questions. Where the question is only part of a *Business of Banking* question, this is indicated at the end, together with the marks allocated to it out of 20.

11.2 The Active Customer

We are concerned here with the type of customer who is very mobile and, maybe, too active to spare the time to visit the bank. He will want his salary paid into an account and to be able to draw cash through an ATM at all hours, wherever he may be. Let us look at this through two questions and outline the possible solutions.

1   Pru Denshul likes to keep a close watch on her bank accounts. She is not able to visit her branch as she spends a lot of time out of the office, keeping in touch usually through her car phone or via her home computer terminal and fax machine (see Figure 11.1).

Figure 11.1   The active customer

What service is available from financial institutions to allow Pru to keep control over her finances? In note form, explain how the system works and give **two** examples of financial institutions that provide such service.

(Part question, 7 marks)

Answer

The service that would most suit Pru's needs is a homebanking service through which she could communicate with the bank by telephone, using a tonepad or voice recognition, or by computer.

She would need to identify herself when making calls to the computer by her PIN number and her account number. She could avail herself of any of the following services:

(a) Make a balance enquiry
(b) Ask for details of recent transactions on the account

(c) Arrange for funds to be transferred
(d) Amend a standing order or direct debit
(e) Ask for a statement
(f) Ask for a cheque book
(g) Arrange to pay a bill

Homebanking facilities are available from several of the High Street banks, from Girobank and from several building societies.

2   Charley Farley is aged 22 and has just left university where he had a basic non-interest-bearing account and a cheque guarantee card. He is keen on keeping up to date with his financial affairs even though he has a job which entails travelling around the country. Charley recently lost his wallet with £200 in it and is now concerned about carrying cash even though he needs to pay some small bills by cash. He runs up quite an expense bill, which he claims back monthly from his employers. Charley is able to save some money each month. Whilst he wants some of the savings to be readily available, £20 a month could be saved on a long-term basis, in order to get capital growth. He lives with his parents but they are driving him mad with their drinking and noisy music.
    List **six** bank services or accounts which you think Charley Farley would find most useful. Explain why each meets his needs.

Answer

(a) Homebanking: this would enable him to communicate about his account on the telephone and to pay some bills that way
(b) An interest-bearing cheque account would enable him to obtain some interest on the savings that he wishes to be accessible
(c) A credit card from the bank's credit card company; this would enable him to pay bills without cash as he travels and provide him with up to 56 days' credit if he pays off the account with one payment each month. He will probably have received reimbursement of his expenses in time to meet these bills
(d) A cheque guarantee/ATM/Switch or Delta card; to support payment of bills by cheque or by electronic means and to be able to draw cash at ATM cashpoints
(e) A personal loan would enable him to buy a car and repay by instalments
(f) Regular monthly investment in a unit trust through the bank should provide for growth in the long term, but it would have to be pointed out to him that the value of units may go down as well as up

A possible seventh service is a house mortgage, preferably with endowment assurance cover, which would enable him to buy a flat or house when he reaches the point where he must leave home.

11.3   Regular Monthly Saving

In assessing the customer's needs concerning regular saving it is necessary to be sure what he (or she) aims to achieve. Is he looking for growth? Is he looking for security as well as growth? Is he looking for a tax-free investment? When is repayment envisaged? How important is accessibility? The following questions and suggested answers will demonstrate this point.

3   Susan Cammel is a lorry driver who has had a pay rise which allows her to save £40 per month. She is aged 42 and will be able to save this amount until she retires. She wants her savings to:
   – give the possibility of significant gains
   – be invested across all sectors of the economy and not be invested in any special sector or country
   – have any returns ploughed back to increase the value of her savings
   What service would you recommend to Susan? Explain how your choice meets her requirements.   (Part question, 7 marks)

Answer

The best monthly investment for Susan would be in a unit trust as this would meet all her specific requirements:

(a) Unit trusts have had a good record of growth in the past and most of them have succeeded in outstripping inflation; however, it would have to be stressed that the value of units can go down as well as up
(b) The risk is spread over a wide range of stocks and/or shares
(c) Susan could choose a general fund rather than one that is specific to a particular sector or country
(d) By choosing Accumulation Units rather than Income Units the dividends would be credited to her in the form of additional units

4   Phyllis Stine can save up to £100 per month and she will not need the money for at least 5 years. Her job is secure and she will be able to save over the whole period. She is a tax payer but does not want to pay tax on her savings.
   What service would you recommend to Phyllis? Explain how the service operates and give two customer benefits.   (Part question, 10 marks)

Answer

The important facts here are that Phyllis does not want to pay tax on her savings and that she wants to invest for a 5-year period. Whilst National Savings Certificates would satisfy both of the needs, there is another product which produces interest tax free and on which the rate of interest would be considerably better, i.e. a TESSA account.

TESSA stands for Tax Exempt Special Savings Account and such accounts are available at the larger banks and building societies. Savings can be made either by monthly instalments or in yearly lump sums up to a maximum of £9,000 over a 5-year period. The maximum investment is £150 per month for regular monthly investments and for lump sums the maximum in Year 1 is £3,000, in Years 2, 3 and 4 £1,800 per year, and in Year 5 £600. The customer's monthly saving is therefore within the limits.

Provided that the interest is left in the account it is free of income tax, but if any withdrawals of interest are made tax has to be deducted. If any of the capital is withdrawn before the end of the 5 years, the right to tax exemption is lost.

Phyllis would benefit from:

(a) Interest that is free of tax
(b) Higher rates of interest than are usually paid by the banks and building societies

Other possible benefits are that some of the institutions pay a bonus at the end of the 5 years if the maximum investment of £3,000 was made in Year 1 (but of course this would not apply to Phyllis), and investors are permitted to transfer their TESSAs from one institution to another to obtain a better rate of interest; some banks and building societies impose a penalty for the work involved.

11.4   Mortgage Finance

When a customer moves house he may require more than a straightforward repayment mortgage because he may have to consider the needs of his family should anything happen to him during the term of the mortgage, and also he may be looking ahead to the time that the mortgage is repaid and he is nearing retirement. He may also require bridging finance.

5   Jack and Jill Hill are aged 35 and 30 respectively and have two young children aged 4 and 2. Jack is a schoolteacher and his wife is a solicitor who has just returned to work.

The Hills are moving house in the near future and will require a mortgage. They are also concerned that they should have a lump sum available when Jack retires. Finally, they want some financial protection for their family should either of them die whilst the children are still young (see Figure 11.2).

Within 2 years Jill will be earning a lot more than Jack and she would like to take out some additional financial protection which would combine saving with protection for their dependants.

What services would you recommend? Give explanations for your choice.

(Part question, 8 marks)

Figure 11.2   Mortgage finance

Answer

The best type of mortgage for the Hills is an Endowment Mortgage over 25 years (by which time Mr Hill will be aged 60). The mortgage will be repaid from the with-profits endowment policy and provide a lump sum, depending upon the amount of the profits, for them at retirement.

To obtain additional protection for the family they could take out a Term Assurance policy, e.g. a Mortgage Protection Policy, which would be relatively cheap.

Jill could take out a straightforward with-profits endowment policy which would provide financial help in bringing up the children should she die, and if not, a lump sum with profits at the maturity of the policy. This policy would also attract a surrender value should it become necessary to redeem it early.

6   Sara and Buster Tendon want to buy their first home: a two bedroomed terraced house. They do not expect to stay there more than 3 years as they both have good careers ahead of them and want eventually to own a detached house. They do not, however, want to keep taking out new mortgages and want to finish making either house payments within 25 years.

What service could allow them to do this? How does it work and what are **two** customer benefits?   (Part question, 5 marks)

Answer

The requirement here is an Endowment Mortgage over 25 years. This involves taking out an endowment policy for the amount of the mortgage and for the period of the mortgage. Interest only is paid on the mortgage and in addition premiums are paid on the assurance policy. The policy provides life cover during the period of the mortgage and, if it is a with-profits policy, a lump sum at maturity as well as repayment of the mortgage.

In addition, the policy provides two benefits which are particularly important in view of the Tendons' requirements. These are that the policy can be transferred to a new mortgage when they move house, and also the term of it can remain unchanged, i.e. 25 years.

11.5 Saving for Retirement

7   Indy Sisive is aged 50 and runs his own company. He is concerned about retirement and wants to place his money so as to ensure that he can enjoy his retirement without having to spend his savings.

What services would you recommend to Indy? Identify another category of person that could use such a service and give one customer benefit.

(Part question, 5 marks)

Answer

The service to be recommended is a personal pension plan. This could be an endowment or unit trust plan and the amounts paid in could vary provided they did not exceed the limit laid down. Other benefits would be that the pension could be transferred to another pension scheme should he give up his company and take up employment, and that the plan provides financial security.

Other categories that would benefit from a private pension plan are sole proprietors, members of a partnership, employees who are not covered by a pension scheme, and persons with second jobs for which there is no pension.

8   Mr I.M. Lucky is aged 50 and has just won £25,000 in a lottery. His job does have a pension plan but he wants to make sure that when he reaches age 60 he will have sufficient income for him to live comfortably. He is prepared to put the money with a company provided that it would pay him a guaranteed income for as long as he lives. He has no family and is not concerned about leaving money to dependants.

Outline a service that would meet his needs.   (Part question, 7 marks)

Answer

The service Mr Lucky requires is a deferred annuity. This would provide him with an income for life from an agreed future date, in return for an investment of a lump sum. As the income will not commence until he is 60 it is a deferred annuity and will attract a higher income because the assurance company has the use of the money for 10 years without having to pay out. Usually the lump sums paid for annuities are not repayable, but in some cases a proportion may be paid back.

Mr Lucky is therefore gambling on living a long time to maximise the benefit from the investment.

Other questions which involve assessing what the customer's requirements are will be found amongst those at the end of previous chapters, where they have been placed in order to illustrate the type of question that might be asked concerning a topic covered in the chapter.

Banking qualifications

12.1 Introduction

The purpose of this chapter is to bring together the facts relating to banking qualifications, not only the range of professional qualifications of the Chartered Institute of Bankers (CIB), but also the new National Vocational Qualifications (NVQs) which are designed to meet the needs of those who wish to be assessed for their practical competence in the bank rather than for their academic knowledge. It is likely that the majority of readers of this book will be studying for *Business of Banking* for the Banking Certificate, and they should therefore be aware of the structure of the CIB examinations; however, it may prove useful to have them summarised here. But for the more general reader it is to be hoped that drawing his or her attention to the qualifications as well as to what banking is all about, may encourage him, or her, to seek employment in banking and to endeavour to become qualified.

This book is also intended for those preparing to be assessed for NVQs at Levels 2 and 3 who will need to study such a text side by side with their practical work to achieve the levels of knowledge and practical competence that will be demanded of them.

12.2 Chartered Institute of Bankers' Examinations

Banking Certificate and Pre-Associateship route

The Banking Certificate is a qualification which caters for the needs of senior supervisory grades and staff who aspire to them. It is meant to be a stand-alone qualification and a certificate is awarded to successful candidates, but it also provides entry for the Associateship examinations. The designatory letters 'Cert. CIB' may be used by holders of the Banking Certificate provided they have had at least 2 years' banking or relevant work experience, have been members of the Chartered Institute of Bankers for at least 2 years and are paid-up members of the Institute.

Selected papers of the Banking Certificate also form the basis of the pre-Associateship Route which provides for speedier progress to the Associate examinations for those with higher entry qualifications. Also, candidates who achieve three merit passes at one sitting in the Preliminary Section of the Banking Certificate may transfer to the Pre-Associateship Route if they wish. Some overseas candidates have local alternative qualifications that are recognised by the Institute for entry purposes.

Entry requirement   For the Preliminary section of the Banking Certificate no entry qualifications are required, but to enter the Final section candidates must have passed the three papers in the Preliminary section or hold a GCE A-Level or equivalent plus GCSE/O-Level English language(Grades A,B or C) or equivalent. Mature students with 5 years' employment in banking or relevant work may be able to gain entry to the Final section without holding formal academic qualifications.

Examination structure   The subjects of the Preliminary and Final sections of the Banking Certificate are as follows:

- Preliminary   Business Calculations
                 Business Communications
                 The Business of Banking
- Final   Economics and the Banks' Role in the Economy
                 Introduction to Accounting
                 Banking; The legal Environment
                 Supervisory Skills
                 Banking Operations – UK Lending and
                     International Business
                 Customer Services – Marketing and the Competitive
                     Environment

The papers may be taken one at a time

Candidates for the pre-Associateship Route are required to pass four papers from the Banking Certificate which must include the first three in the Final section plus one of the remaining three. Candidates must pass all four papers in a maximum of three consecutive attempts.

The Banking Certificate examinations are held twice a year in May and October.

Associateship examinations

The Associateship examinations form the recommended qualification for the majority of career bankers. Successful candidates are entitled to use the designatory letters 'ACIB'.

Entry requirements   To be eligible to sit the examinations candidates must have passed the Banking Certificate, the pre-Associateship Route (or the old Foundation Course) or other recognised qualification acceptable to the Chartered Institute. Alternatively, they must hold a recognised degree or professional qualification of a standard and content acceptable to the Institute, and they may be able to obtain exemption from some of the subjects, but normally this is restricted to the core subjects. All candidates must be members of the Institute.

Examination structure   Candidates must take the four core papers and any four option papers. The subjects are as follows:

- Core papers   Law Relating to Banking Services
                 The Monetary and Financial System
                 Accountancy
                 Management in Banking
- Option papers Administration of Estates
                 Administration of Trusts
                 Banking Operations – Regulation, Market
                     Practice and Treasury Management
                 Branch Banking – Law and Practice
                 Corporate Banking – Practice and Law
                 Information Technology
                 Investment
                 Lending
                 Marketing
                 Multinational Corporate Finance
                 Offshore Practice and Administration
                 Taxation
                 Trade Finance – Payments and Services

Certain combinations of option subjects are recommended for Trustee students, those concerned with corporate/international services, and those involved in retail banking. The actual choice depends upon the candidate's career plans and personal preferences.

Students are advised to take two and not more than three subjects at a sitting, but they may take each paper singly and in any sequence provided that the examination timetable allows.

As for the Certificate, examinations are held twice-yearly in May and October.

The Lombard Scheme

This scheme provides an opportunity for Associates of the Chartered Institute of Bankers to proceed further with their studies at postgraduate level. They study for a Master's degree in Business Administration (MBA) at one of six major UK business schools. After completion of the taught part of the course successful candidates are entitled to use the designatory letters 'DipFS', provided specified financial services subjects have been taken. When the entire course has been successfully completed, the MBA is awarded by the business school concerned.

12.3   National Vocational Qualifications in Banking

National Vocational Qualifications (NVQs) are qualifications that set the standards for occupational and professional competence and they are based on practical performance rather than academic performance. They are made up of units and each unit sets out in detail the standards to be achieved and the performance criteria. Credits for units can be achieved separately over time.

The National Council for Vocational Qualifications was set up with the backing of the government, the Confederation of British Industry and the Trades Union Council, to develop this new system of qualifications to meet the needs of trainees for whom purely academic courses would be inappropriate. This applies particularly, though not only, to young trainees, to women returning to work and to older workers, both full- and part-time. The intention is to develop and modernise occupational training to enable companies and their employees to raise the level of performance and create greater mobility of the workforce.

For each industry Lead Bodies have been established that have responsibility for setting performance standards at a number of levels and for working out assessment procedures for the award of NVQs. The Banking Lead Body comprises representatives from a number of banks, the Chartered Institute of Bankers and the Chartered Institute of Bankers in Scotland, representatives of employees in banking, and persons from each of the government bodies most concerned. Its secretariat is located at the Banking Information Service at 10 Lombard Street, London. The awarding bodies are the Chartered Institute of Bankers and the City and Guilds of London Institute.

In November 1992 the Level 2 Banking Services qualification was accredited by the National Council for Vocational Qualifications. This qualification consisted of 7 mandatory units and 5 optional units (any 2 optional units required to complete the qualification). Seven of these units were banking-specific and included banking tasks such as processing vouchers, sales, counter service, foreign exchange, etc.; the remainder of the units were taken from the Administration Lead Body standards. A full pilot was carried out during 1992 and an evaluation was undertaken and completed early 1993. The Level 2 was substantially revised following recommendations from the evaluation. The new Level 2 qualification is skills-based rather than task-based and consists of 6 mandatory units and 3 optional units. The Lead Body are working towards its accreditation by Spring 1994.

Although employees are assessed by observation of performance at the workplace and by oral questions by the assessor, who is likely to be their supervisor, there are nevertheless areas of related knowledge in the Level 2 NVQ which could best be acquired by reference to a textbook such as this one. It is to be hoped, therefore, that participants will wish to back up their practical training by reading at least parts of this book and that their appetites for further study and for written examinations will be whetted.

Levels 3 and 4

The Lead Body is making good progress with the development of NVQs at Levels 3 and 4 and it is likely that they will be put forward for accreditation by spring 1994. The Level 3 NVQ is considered by the Lead Body to equate to the Banking Certificate and Level 4 (and Level 5 when it is eventually prepared) to the Associateship. The contents of all of these NVQs will include aspects of lending, taking securities, foreign business and of administration, management and selling, and will therefore call for a great deal of study as well as practical application. *Mastering Banking* will supply the knowledge input at Level 3 because the Business of Banking syllabus, which it is designed to cover, equates to what the bank officer at that level needs to know if he is to be competent in his practical work.

Index